THE SAVIOR
Beyond the Storms

STEPHEN SELESTINO

ISBN 979-8-88644-233-5 (Paperback)
ISBN 979-8-88644-240-3 (Hardcover)
ISBN 979-8-88644-234-2 (Digital)

Covenant Books
11661 Hwy 707
Murrells Inlet, SC 29576
www.covenantbooks.com

INTRODUCTION

Life for me began with difficulty. I was adopted at the age of three months. Born in San Antonio, Texas, I was accepted into the Selestino family of Lockhart, Texas. My grandfather knew someone, who knew someone, who found out about my biological mother, Delia Guzman, and her financial crisis. Delia could not afford to financially sustain my needs, which is how the verbal adoption presented itself.

It would be years later that my sister Terri said that my biological sister was screaming and yelling, "*No*! Don't take my little brother away! Please, Mom, don't let them take my brother!" The incident must have been traumatizing for Terri, as a little girl then. To watch my biological sister agonizing while the Selestino family took me from the Guzman family. As far as Delia was concerned, I was told that she did not want to give me up, but she felt she had no choice.

I came into the Selestino family a filthy, dirty baby. I was screaming with terrible earaches and unchanged diapers. Rash galore! I was immediately sent for medical treatment due to my unhealthy condition. My eyes were filled with gunk, and my ears needed to be gently cleaned. The slightest touch would set me off.

It was unbelievable to my stepmother, Maria Selestino, the condition I was in. She did her utmost to tend to all my ailments and find fast medical solutions. She wanted me to have some semblance of healing and comfort. I am sure she wanted my screaming to stop as well.

I have always considered Santiago Selestino my *real* dad. I do remember in my later years my dad telling me that Delia came to see me when I was five years old. Why did I not see her? Why did I miss the opportunity of seeing my *real* mother? Did my dad prevent Delia from seeing me? Did my dad argue with her and told her to get lost? Why was I not allowed to see her?

The answer was twofold. First, the Selestino family did not want to let me go. After they had sacrificed their efforts, love, and responsibility to me, now I was going to be taken from them. Dad was afraid and heartbroken. How would he tell Mom, Maria, and Terri that I would be given back to Delia? I honestly believe that it broke my dad's heart that I would no longer be a part of their lives. I also think that my dad recognized how devastated my mom and sister Terri would be.

Secondly, Dad told me that he and Delia talked. Dad said that Delia commented that she wanted to take me back. He told Delia that if she took me back, she would not ever bring me to the Selestino family again. He told Delia he was not going to be playing this "I will take him home…I have to bring him back again" game. Dad made it clear to Delia that the Selestino family loved me, and they were *not* going to have their hearts ripped out over and over again.

Dad told Delia, "If you take him, you better make sure that you can support him. If you bring him back again, we will not take him in again!" Delia did not remove me from the Selestino family, and she was never heard from again.

I had always pondered the question in my heart: why did Mom give me up? I took it very personally. Even though the answer had already been provided, I was blinded by rejection. For so long I was resentful for what she did. I was angry and bitter. As a young boy, that resentment came out in various ways—very destructive and violent ways.

It wasn't until later in life that God opened my eyes, and I was able to see the truth for what it was; it was not personal but rather survival. Had I remained in San Antonio, Texas, I probably would not have survived the condition that I was in.

As I grew older, I was a normal youth in my hometown. Dad was a construction laborer, and Mom and Terri worked as maids in Austin. They worked hard to maintain our homelife.

Mom was a wonderful cook. When I was a boy, the smell of chorizo (Mexican sausage) would wake me up on Saturday mornings. Along with the smell of fresh homemade tortillas that complimented eggs, chunks of crispy potatoes, and refried beans, it was an incredible way to wake up. Mom's tortillas were hot enough that I would grab a stick of butter, rub it on the tortilla, and watch as the butter melted as I enjoyed devouring the treat.

Dad would take us on vacation every year to Corpus Christi in the summer. I loved going to carnivals, Fourth of July festivals, and the San Antonio Zoo. Life was just not worth living if we didn't go to the zoo.

Years went by and I went from youth to teen, in what seemed like a very short span of time. Before I knew it, I was graduating from Lockhart High School in the early summer of 1984. From there, I was lost. High school provided guidance, direction, and instruction. I had something to look forward to; I had a purpose. I always had an outline of what needed to be done.

Discipline taught me that if deadlines were not met, there would be consequences. Now I was on my own. No more teachers to turn to. No more classes that required research to find answers. No more deadlines to turn homework in. No more projects that sometimes required weekend time. The reality of real life was beginning, and I had no concept of what to do next. I would have to learn how to find my way.

My adulthood began with the nightlife. This is where my life took a downward spiral. From the age of twenty-one to thirty, I was an alcoholic and very promiscuous. I had discovered that alcohol would numb the pains I had felt, and different women meant I could have fun without responsibility or commitment. I would become an embarrassment to my family. I was clearly headed for hell, *real* fast.

As the years went by, the storms grew in intensity. Spiritually speaking, I did not have a clue as to how to take shelter from the storms. I had no concept or knowledge of God, Jesus, and the Holy Spirit. I only had parental and street advice.

I will never forget Betty Brown. God had put Betty in my life for the purpose of coming to him. Betty led me to Christ. I wish I could say that I did a 180, but I didn't. I would continue on that destructive path. It would not be until my latter years that the power of the Almighty God would manifest itself in many different ways.

God's love, grace, and mercy is so miraculous and awesome. So awesome that he would one day open my eyes to see in ways that are too wonderful for words.

God opened my eyes to see Jesus Christ, the Savior beyond the storms!

PROLOGUE

In the book of Matthew 14:15–21, Jesus fed a crowd of five thousand people. This was an incredible miracle because the disciples had just told Jesus that there were only five loaves of bread and two fish.

In verses 22–33, Jesus instructed his disciples to get into a boat, go before him, and get to the other side. Jesus stayed behind to disperse the crowd. After the crowd left, Jesus then went to a mountain and prayed. As the night came, Jesus was alone.

The story goes on to say that the ship was now in the middle of the sea. The disciples were in one of the most horrible storms. The waves were tossing the vessel out in the middle of the sea.

Then came one of the most told accounts in all of Christianity. Verse 25 says, "And in the fourth watch of the night Jesus went unto them, WALKING <u>ON</u> THE SEA" (emphasis mine). Jesus was literally walking on the sea *during* a violent storm.

The Matthew Henry Bible commentary says it this way:

> This is a great instance of Christ's sovereign dominion over all the creatures; they are all under his feet, and at his command; they forget their natures, and change the qualities that we call essential. We need not enquire how this was done, whether by condensing the surface of the water (when God pleases, the depths are congealed in the heart of the sea, Exodus 15:8), or by suspending the gravitation of his body, which was transfigured as he pleased; it is sufficient that it proves his divine power, for it is God's preroga-

tive to tread upon the waves of the sea (Job 9:8), as it is to ride upon the wings of the wind.

In one of the most critical time of their lives, Jesus came to disciples walking on the sea. The Bible says that the disciples were troubled. So here are the disciples on a ship, doing what they were told to do; trying to get to the other side. While in the middle of the sea, they are tossed about by a fierce storm. Now the problem is compounded by them seeing a *spirit* coming to them, walking on the sea. I would venture to guess that their hearts were pounding inside their scared little chests.

"Be of good cheer; it is I; be not afraid," Jesus said.

Peter was bold enough to speak despite his fear. "Lord, if it be thou, bid me come unto thee on the water."

Jesus responded, "Come."

When Peter stepped out of the boat, he too was walking on the sea. Peter was focused on his Lord. There was no denying his trust in Christ; the evidence of him walking on the sea testified to his faith.

Then Peter began to take his eyes off Christ. Peter heard the boisterous wind blowing around him, and he became afraid. His focus shifted from Christ to the chaos surrounding him. He began to sink into the sea. It was Peter's sense of imminent peril that caused him to cry, "Lord, save me."

The Bible says that Christ did three things; first, Jesus "immediately stretched forth his hand." Second, Jesus caught him. Lastly, Jesus spoke to Peter, saying, "O thou of little faith, wherefore didst thou doubt?" The point? Jesus saw Peter's faith. There was no way Jesus was going to let Peter perish. All it takes utilizing that *measure of faith* we have been given.

The Matthew Henry Bible commentary says:

He saved him; *he answered him with the saving strength of his right hand* (Psalm 20:6), for immediately *he stretched forth his hand, and caught him*. Note, Christ's time to save is when we sink (Psalm 18:4–7): he helps at a deadlift. Christ's hand is still stretched out to all believers, to keep them from sinking. Those whom he hath once apprehended as his own, and hath snatched as *brands out of the burning*, he will catch out of the water too. Though he may seem to have left his hold, he doth but seem to do so, for they shall *never perish, neither shall any man pluck them out of his hand* (John 10:28). Never fear, he will hold his own. Our deliverance from our own fears, which else would overwhelm us, is owing to the hand of his power and grace (Psalm 34:4).

The completion of the miracle came when both Jesus and Peter entered the boat (Matthew 14:32); "the wind ceased." The storm was over.

No one in life has it easy. God never intended life to be easy. Life is full of storms. Storms range from hurricanes to tornadoes, earthquakes, lightning storms, typhoons, and tsunamis. When the storms cease, we are left to rebuild and start our lives over again. That analogy corresponds to our spiritual storms as well.

When God permits the storms, it is to build our spiritual strength and to put our dependence on Him. Just as Jesus knew his disciples would face that dreadful storm, I have learned that God has allowed horrific storms in my life. Like his disciples, his timing was perfect. Just before I went under, he caught my hand and took me in.

I have written this book for three reasons:

First, to honor God, Jesus Christ, and the Holy Spirit.

I have prayed for the publishing of this book as a testimony of God's incredible faithfulness, God's unfailing love, and God's limitless power. Over and over again, God has demonstrated his kindness, mercy, forgiveness, and patience for all the wrongs I have done. God has been there to pick me up when I have been wronged.

Christ has overcome the world. This is where I have drawn strength. In writing this book, I knew I would face old challenges again. I had to relive some of those terrible moments—embarrassing, humiliating, and painful moments I thought I would never have to face again. Because Jesus rose from the dead, it was he who resurrected me from my past.

The Holy Spirit of God has inspired me, encouraged me, and guided me through every word to be as detailed as I can recall. He gave me the courage to press on for a greater purpose than myself.

As you will see, my past will testify against me. I am not without guilt. I was that guy that was very insolent, uncaring, thoughtless, and self-centered. This is the motivation I need to follow through with this book. To *step out*, reach for the Savior, and hopefully give you, the reader, hope.

Second, inspiration.

Having gone through some terrifying experiences, my hope and prayer are that you will be inspired to see God's incredible grace. The inspiration that says, "If your life was that two-thousand-piece jigsaw puzzle that was scattered by a hurricane, cast your cares on God because he loves you. God is able to put your life back together again!"

That inspiration brings hope where there was none. When everything seemed so abysmal, God will be with you and walk with you till the very end. My inspiration was that God walked with me every step of the way. Every time I came out on the other side, God was still with me.

Jesus is the light of the world. I pray that if you are suffering in darkness, no matter the circumstances you are facing, you will let Jesus be that light that inspires you to continue on. Press on; even if it means that you grind your teeth and strap your boots on tight, don't stop. Jesus is the only way to safety.

Lastly, encouragement.

Suffering is very painful. At times it seems, no one is around or no one cares. It could be that you have messed up so bad, there is no hope of getting back. Did someone abandon you? Did someone cause you traumatic pain? Have you lost trust in someone? Did you hurt someone? Did you walk away when you should have stayed? Are you in a dark place? Is your situation so bad that you are contemplating suicide?

I pray that you will be encouraged to turn to God in your most vulnerable moments. I hope that you will see how God brought me out of all these serious questions. I share some profound moments of my life so that you may not despair or give up.

Some of my most vulnerable moments are the following:

- At the age of ten, I suffered sexual abuse in front of four people.
- While still at the age of ten, I would rebel against my mom and be struck by a car that almost cost me my life.
- My addiction to alcohol. How I was so stupid driving drunk to the point of passing out behind the wheel, almost killing others and myself.
- My addiction to promiscuity. I now bear the consequences of being so promiscuous that it has had life-altering implications.
- Almost dying due to COVID I caught SARS pneumonia and was in ICU for over a month. After ICU, I spent another two weeks in a regular hospital room, trying to strengthen my lungs from the adverse effects of SARS. After that, I spent another twelve days at Encompass Health in Columbia, South Carolina, learning to rebuild my strength so that I could return home.

After making a mess of my finances and relationships and his will for my life, only God was able to restore what I had destroyed. Through it all, salvation has come by the grace of God, through Jesus Christ and the power of his Holy Spirit.

God has taken the most painful, humiliating, and embarrassing moments in my life and has encouraged me to reach out to others. When God walks with you through your storms, you will come out on the other side as refined gold. You too will have *his* strength to encourage others. The weakness that once you hid in the dark will one day be the strong saving grace, in Christ, to rescue someone from drowning.

Through suffering and pain, joy and laughter, sunshine and rain, may this book honor God.

- May God richly bless you (Ephesians 1:3);
- May God keep you (2 Thessalonians 3:3 and Jude 1:24);
- May God open your eyes and show you his love (John 3:16 and Romans 8:38–39); and
- May the grace of God always be with you (2 John 1:3)!

CHAPTER 1

Ten, a Difficult Age
Part One: Sexual Assault

The year was 1976.

Dad had just placed our brand-new, single-wide mobile home on an acre of land in Lockhart, Texas. So much work still needed to be done on the property. There was so much brush to be cleared from the backyard. Our new driveway needed a path. Trash needed to be picked up. Branches strewn all over the yard needed to be put in a pile so that city maintenance could dispose of them. Rusty old barbed wire fencing needed to be gathered and carried away to the dump.

After living in a small house just around the corner, we were all excited to be in our new home. A single-wide mobile home was a mansion in comparison to the old house we had. It was ours, and we loved it. It was home.

After moving all our stuff into our new home, Terri and I were excited about having our own rooms. Separate rooms. Since I was three months, I always slept with Terri. Now the time had come to go our own way, so to speak. I was afraid at first, but it didn't take long to find our own space.

I marveled at the size of our living room. To me it was incredible. The TV looked so small in comparison to the small house with the big TV. I couldn't wait to see my shows in our new living room.

She burst out onto the television screen as Pepper Anderson. She was so incredibly beautiful. I was in love. Sergeant Anderson was an undercover police officer working for the Criminal Conspiracy Unit of the Los Angeles Police Department. She was tough, and she was blond. Pepper went undercover (as a prostitute, nurse, teacher, flight attendant, prison inmate, dancer, waitress, etc.) to get close enough to the suspects to gain valuable information that would lead to their arrest. She was Angie Dickinson in *Police Woman*.

"Steve Austin, astronaut. A man barely alive. We can rebuild him. We have the technology. We can make him better than he was. Better, stronger, faster." Astronaut Steve Austin was severely injured in the crash of an experimental lifting body aircraft. He is "rebuilt" in an operation that costs $6 million. His right arm, both legs, and left eye are replaced with *bionic* implants that enhance his strength, speed, and vision far above human norms; he can run at speeds of over sixty miles per hour. Lee Majors was *The Six Million Dollar Man*.

"Love, exciting and new. Come Aboard. We're expecting you. And Love, life's sweetest reward. Let it flow, it floats back to you..." Captain Merrill Stubing (Gavin MacLeod), Gopher (Fredrick Lawrence Grandy), Julie McCoy (Lauren Tewes), Doc Adam Bricker (Bernie Kopell), and bartender Isaac Washington (Ted Lange) were always ready to welcome you on *The Love Boat*. I think half the time I wasn't interested in the story line. I was more interested in Julie.

The evenings would find Terri and I watching these shows together. Not to mention that life was not complete without the annual showing of *The Wizard of Oz* and *The Ten Commandments*.

Saturday nights were taken. First, it was *The Dick Van Dyke Show*, followed by *The Love Boat*, and the night came to an end after *Fantasy Island*. Terri would make some snacks. Whether it was mac and cheese, hot dogs, popcorn, or even some of Mom's leftover cooking. I couldn't wait for Saturday nights with my sister. It wasn't hard to see how close my sister and I were.

After school let out the summer of 1976, I was looking forward to my vacation days that were ahead. I had a good Huffy bicycle. I had my dog Tuffy, and I had a limitless amount of energy. Tuffy was a beautiful German shepherd and collie mix. Times were good. A boy and his dog wandering around the forest behind his house, exploring the creeks and savoring the wild green grapes.

Tuffy was such an incredible dog. Very faithful. All I would have to do is say "Sick 'em, Tuffy!" and he was gone after whatever dog came into his view. He would never allow another dog to come near me. If you were daring enough to harass me, Tuffy would let you know to back off. His pearly white canines were no joke.

Our family, minus Dad, would visit relatives in California. The road trips were long, hot, and boring. The trips generally lasted for two weeks. When I got tired, I couldn't wait to get back to my dog. I couldn't wait to run around with my dog.

When we came home, Dad would tell me that Tuffy would be howling for me when I wasn't home. "That dog really misses you," he would say. It never failed; the reunion brought cuts and scratches from all the excitement Tuffy showed when I returned home.

The summers in Texas were really hot. Tuffy and I went swimming in the local creeks. It was a good way to cool off from the Texas heat and high humidity. Me and Tuffy splashing around without a care in the world.

Life was simple. The innocence of a ten-year-old boy thrived with his family and his dog.

That innocence would be interrupted with one devastating act.

Our creeks were good places to dig up worms for fishing trips. Within a matter of minutes, you could dig up enough worms to make it a day of fishing. Clothing, shoes, hands, and face covered in mud. It was okay because all you had to do is take a jump in the nearby creek and rinse off. No biggie!

On this particular day, I was with two friends and two cousins. Tuffy had stayed at home on this day. The five of us had planned on going fishing at our local city park a couple of miles away. We would dig up some worms, rush home to get our fishing rods and reels, and we would meet up at the park.

Just as we had started to walk away, I felt a piercing jab on my back. Thinking I had gotten stung by a bee, I turned to swat it away. It was then that I felt a hand on my right shoulder and the painful jab still there. A voice said, "Go down to the creek, or I will cut you." I thought this was a joke that my friends were playing on me. As I went to turn around, the hand forced me to remain facing forward.

"Don't turn around, or I'll stab you!" he said.

I said, "Let me see the knife."

I felt the piercing jab subside. He brought his hand around and showed me a midsize silver pocketknife. The piercing jab was back. I was now terrified and in shock as I knew this was real!

All six of us went down to the part of the creek where the tunnel was. It was near the area where we would dig for worms. The creek ran through a tunnel beneath the road above. The creek was at an angle that no one driving above could see down to the creek.

I was forced to take all my clothes off. Right there in front of everyone to see. I instantly felt fear. The kind of fear that drowns out life around you. I had no sense of hearing, seeing, and smelling. It was as though I was in a vacuum. In a confined prison of fear without bars. Disassociated from everything and everyone.

At one point, I remember looking up to see four young boys looking on as I was being assaulted and humiliated. The thought of running didn't come into my thoughts; I was too afraid. Afraid that if he caught me, he would take me out.

I do not remember how long the assault occurred. It felt like forever.

"Why are you doing this?" I asked.

"Shut up or I'll kill you!" he responded.

To this day, I believe that my friends and my cousins were too afraid to get involved. They were in shock. They were powerless. All they could do was to look on. So much so that no one thought of leaving to call for police.

What he did, to say the least, was shameful and devastating.

Then, he stopped and took off running.

I remember just standing there, feeling all alone and overcome by fear. What do I do? I instinctively put my clothes back on. After we all gathered ourselves and came to our senses, we all left and went to a church close to where I lived.

"Should I call the police?" I asked.

"No, because if *he* finds out, he will kill you," they said. Even after the incident, there was still that sense of dread lingering.

"I'm just going to go home," I said. "I want to take a shower and get clean."

Nothing could remove the shame, degradation, humiliation, and despair that I felt. A thousand showers could not remove the filth. I never forgot the numbness I felt.

"Okay," they said. "Take care."

I believe that they felt genuine sorrow for what had just happened. Because they were young and horrified, they didn't know how to offer help. I have no doubt they felt helpless.

As I walked home, I remember saying to myself, *I can't tell Mom and Dad. How horrible it would be if anyone found out about this. If I said anything, I would bring shame to my family. I don't want Mom and Dad to be the laughingstock of Lockhart! Don't embarrass them like this. Just keep it to yourself. What did I do that made him do this? Did I say something wrong? I should have never planned on going fishing! If I had just stayed home, this would not have happened!*

Never mind what just happened to me. Never mind the feeling of worthlessness. Never mind the trauma.

I thought that the horrific nightmare would just go away. I can keep it inside, and no one has to know. I would begin living a lie.

Summer, winter, fall, and spring, it was still there. Sunny days and cloudy days, it was still there. No matter how far I went with my family, it tagged along. At family outings, at carnivals, at the movies, on vacation; there was no escaping the trauma.

To describe the torment was next to impossible. How does a ten-year-old boy explain what he had just experienced? Chances are, you are not going to hear much from him. I liken that kind of fear as a firm grip around the throat. The unseen hand that controlled my ability to have a choice. How difficult is it to talk about the assault? Impossible! To me, it would have been more like an interrogation than it would be someone trying to help me. I didn't know how to talk about it without the feeling of someone using the occurrence against me. It was devastating.

As a young boy, my dad and I were close. We went fishing together. We took trips together. I recall taking a trip to Mexico together. We always watched our beloved Dallas Cowboys together. We would shoot his .22-caliber rifle frequently. We had a close bond, and I loved the closeness we shared.

After being molested, our bond was shattered. I no longer trusted my dad. A broken ten-year-old boy became distant from his dad.

The fishing trips were done. The moments when we would go swimming at Five Mile Dam in Kyle, Texas were over. No more museums. No more trips to the coast. The dad-and-son moments were a thing of the past. If no one else went with us, I wasn't going anywhere with my dad alone. Why? It wasn't Dad's fault.

I recall Dad asking me, "Why don't we ever go anywhere together anymore?"

The question terrified me. It also brought sadness. It terrified me because I didn't want him to find out about *that*. It was sad because I knew he was missing the father-and-son moments. I was too. I ran from him when he expressed concern. I never gave him a chance after that. This is where I learned how to run from my problems.

Dad, you need to back off! I can't let you get close to me anymore! I can only love you from a distance! Just stay over there. When I feel I can trust you, I will approach you. This was my attitude. I had always hoped that he would never find out.

"I don't know Dad," I would answer. I was lying. I knew the answer. How do you tell your dad, "*I don't trust you, Dad*"? I sure as heck was not going to tell him what happened. I was becoming more and more tormented and confused. I had no idea that the assault was not my fault. I certainly wasn't about to let anyone get close enough to help me figure it out. I was too afraid.

I would quickly dart off so that I wouldn't have to face the question again. I was so scared that I didn't want to feel like I was obligated to explain what happened that terrible day.

In my young adult life, I had become an alcoholic. Now, I was an embarrassment to my family. So now I am carrying the assault and the guilt as well as knowing that I was the *bad apple* of my family.

Yet the overwhelming urge to tell my dad was undeniable. Eleven years of keeping it in had reached its finale.

On a particular Saturday night, I was intoxicated. I decided I was going to my dad's house to tell him what had happened to me years ago. How horrible to say that it took me being under the influence of alcohol to reach out to him. How horrible it was that I loved my dad so much but I didn't trust him enough to say anything about it. Until now.

"Dad, I have something to tell you," is how I started.

Here I was, standing in front of the man that I cherished. The man that took me into this family and loved me as his own. The man that I had pushed away and shunned for fear. The man that I had no longer trusted. This was the same man that tonight I would reach out to in hopes that he would not disown me.

"What, *mijo*?" Dad said. *Mijo* [*me-ho*] is a Hispanic term of endearment meaning *son*.

My first train of thought was that my dad was thinking, *Here he comes, drunk again. What does he want now?*

I felt the fear of rejection rearing its ugly head. Would he be embarrassed of me? Would he disown me like Delia did? Would he say, *"Get out of my house!"* One particular voice said, *"You're not stupid enough to tell him, are you? All that your dad has done for you and this is how you are going to treat him? You have the audacity to stand in front of your dad—the dad that took you in, the dad that has loved you all these years—and you're going to shatter him like this?"*

After the traumatic experience, it was so easy for me to believe a lie than it was to believe the truth. For me, it was a coping mechanism. It was easier for me to be ready to be rejected than to believe that I was not and not be prepared for it.

"Dad, when I was ten, I was sexually molested." I actually said it! I was overwhelmed. Eleven years of holding it all in finally came out. I was broken and tired. Tired of being afraid of my own dad.

"I was so afraid all these years to say anything to you because I didn't want to embarrass you. I know how much people love you, and I didn't want you to be embarrassed in front of your friends! I'm so sorry, Dad, so sorry!" As the tears ran down my face, I was too overwhelmed to speak anymore. I stood in front of the man that I loved so much. What would he say? I could only hope that he wouldn't push me away.

"*Mijo*," he said. "YOU ARE MY SON! I love you! I'm not embarrassed of you. I'm proud of you! I am proud to be your dad, *mijo*. Don't ever forget that!"

What? You mean Dad still loves me?

Dad embraced me. I looked at him and saw him crying as well.

"It's okay," he said. I *really* believed him.

For the first time in a long time, I felt acceptance! If there is one thing I can say with absolute certainty, is that the words of my dad were so needed. I stood in awe of his much-needed affirmation and consolation.

Dad was a sickly man the latter years of his life. As the seasons changed, he was always in the hospital because of chronic asthma. His lungs were so sensitive to pollen and mold. He never left home without his inhaler. When I did go see him, the loud *crackling* sounds coming from his lungs let me know that he was struggling to breathe. It hurt me to my core to see him suffer like that.

In late March of 1998, we had to take him to the hospital. Doctors ran tests on him. It wasn't long before finding out that Dad had tumors in his lymph nodes. Doctors recommended chemotherapy. With chemo, Dad had possibly two to three years to live. Without it, Dad had, at best, three months. Dad said no. Dad made it clear that he was not going to live out the remainder of his life sick from radiation.

I was working at a plastic plant. The phone rang over the intercom system.

"Stephen! It's for you!" the team leader shouted.

I already knew. Terri's voice said, "Dad is dying."

"I'm on the way," I said.

I got to his house. Terri was there and my other sister, Rosa. I looked at Dad lying on his medical bed. His body gasping for air. How I wanted to have one more conversation with him. To say, "I love you, Dad" and him being able to receive it. To hear "I love you, *mijo*" just one more time!

We were all raised Catholic. I had come to Christ in 1989/1990-ish. What kept me together was that I had spoken to Dad about the Gospel. Two weeks prior, Dad had received Jesus as his Lord. That was such an incredible moment. Dad had actually asked Christ to be his Lord and Savior and to forgive him of all his sins.

God had given me peace as I watched him lying there. Then he stopped breathing; Dad was gone.

"Thank you, God," I prayed. "Thank you for giving me a wonderful dad. I'm gonna miss him. Thank you for all the moments we shared and for the time I did spend with him. Thank you, Lord, for giving me the opportunity to tell him about you, Jesus. God, please bless him as he comes into your presence. In Jesus's name I pray, amen!"

So there we stood, two men crying. This was a pivotal moment in my life. If my dad had rejected me, I don't know what I would have done. Since my biological mother had cast me aside, and now my dad was too, what reason or purpose would I have for continuing on?

I had really believed that the possibility existed that Dad would shun me away as I did him. He didn't! Again, my dad took me in.

I had come to regret that I had pushed Dad away. Forgiving myself would not come easy or anytime soon.

Little did I realize that my *real* Father was watching!

> The LORD is watching everywhere, keeping
> his eye on both the evil and the good.
>
> —Proverbs 15:3 (NLT)

CHAPTER 2

God's Providence
Surviving Sexual Assault

From zero to one hundred miles an hour in an instant. I went from being a carefree and innocent ten-year-old to constantly looking over my shoulders, looking at everyone with suspicion. Waiting for that sudden move or that sudden look that meant trouble so that I could run the other way. Waiting for a word that would trigger a certain response, causing me to put that person in a negative light. I trusted no one.

Trust was broken in faith, family, and friends. From having healthy relationships to none.

Sadly, I didn't even consider praying to God because I didn't know how, and I didn't think God cared. To me, God was *way* up there, and I was *way* down here. I didn't consider God at the age of ten. If anything, God was a fleeting thought. Why would he listen to me? Even if he did, he wouldn't help me.

As much as I loved my sister Terri, I was too afraid to tell her. Terri never gave me any reason not to trust her, but I was too scared to speak.

As much as I wanted to say something to my mother, I was not able to trust her; I could not afford to have her say something to someone, to find that I would have to pay another hefty price for something that wasn't my fault.

I sure as heck didn't trust my friends to *keep it a secret*. When I entered high school, the two "friends" that were there that terrible day spread the news. The secret came out. I was ridiculed and made fun of. I denied every bit of it.

The one relationship that I cherished most and that meant everything to me was that between my dad and me. This is the one relationship that really tore me up inside. At first, I only cared about not embarrassing him. To me, the last thing he needed to hear was, "Hey, Chago, your kid's a loser." Chago was a name that his friends called him. I was not about to put him through that. That was my thought process.

I missed my dad; I missed *our time*. The less time I spent with him, the angrier I became. Over the years, I would be so exasperated because it was like my dad was here, but he wasn't around. Even though I was the one pushing him away. This concept was not something this ten-year-old boy knew or understood.

I was confused, hurt, and broken, and I didn't trust anyone. I wanted to speak, but I didn't know how. I was emotionally tormented. I hated what was done to me; and eventually, I hated myself. I was becoming more and more of a recluse. It was hopeless. There was no way out.

To be quite honest, the only one I trusted was my dog, Tuffy. He was the only one that I could say whatever I wanted, and it would stay between us. Tuffy would not judge, ridicule, make fun of, or degrade me. He loved me just the way I was. He didn't care; he would stand beside me through it all.

I was now a ten-year-old boy incarcerated in a prison with no bars. A prisoner of sexual assault and degradation.

The sexual abuse that I experienced had negative effects in my life. Abusers never consider the ramifications of their actions; I don't think they care! It's all about their perverted, pedophiliac appetites.

I pray for all those children who have suffered at the hands of abusers. The innocent pays a heavy price. It is only by God's powerful grace that we pull through.

This is one of my primary purposes for writing this book—that God would touch the heart of someone who has or is currently experiencing this diabolical act.

In researching some resources for you, the reader, I have found that most states use the following organization for their primary source of help: the National Sexual Assault Hotline (800.656.4673). Their website is https://www.rainn.org/.

The following information I have provided in this chapter are statistics that was beneficial for me. I hope that it will be helpful for those who are or have been sexually assaulted and violated in any way!

Sexual abuse is so debilitating that while one can survive it, it is more reasonable to get help. That help can come from family members and loved ones; however, it is equally important to receive help from medical and counseling professionals. Don't go it alone; there is help waiting to assist you!

We are not alone!

David Finkelhor is the director of the Crimes against Children Research Center, codirector of the Family Research Laboratory, and professor of sociology at the University of New Hampshire.

He has also written about child homicide, missing and abducted children, children exposed to domestic and peer violence, and other forms of family violence. To his credit, he has authored eleven books and over 150 journal articles and book chapters. He has received grants from the National Institute of Mental Health, the National Center on Child Abuse and Neglect, and the US Department of Justice. In 1994, he was given the Distinguished Child Abuse Professional Award by the American Professional Society on the Abuse of Children, and in 2004, he was given the Significant Achievement Award from the Association for the Treatment of Sexual Abusers (http://www.unh.edu/ccrc/researchers/finkelhor-david.html).

In a National Center for Victims of Crime article, it stated:

The prevalence of child sexual abuse is difficult to determine because it is often not reported; experts agree that the incidence is far greater than what is reported to authorities. CSA is also not uniformly defined, so statistics may vary. Statistics below represent some of the research done on child sexual abuse.

The U.S. Department of Health and Human Services' Children's Bureau report *Child Maltreatment 2010* found that 9.2% of victimized children were sexually assaulted (page 24).

Studies by David Finkelhor, Director of the Crimes Against Children Research Center, show that:

- 1 in 5 girls and 1 in 20 boys is a victim of child sexual abuse;
- Self-report studies show that 20% of adult females and 5–10% of adult males recall a childhood sexual assault or sexual abuse incident;
- During a one-year period in the U.S., 16% of youth ages 14 to 17 had been sexually victimized;
- Over the course of their lifetime, 28% of U.S. youth ages 14 to 17 had been sexually victimized;
- Children are most vulnerable to CSA between the ages of 7 and 13.

According to a 2003 National Institute of Justice report, 3 out of 4 adolescents who have been sexually assaulted were victimized by someone they knew well (page 5).

A Bureau of Justice Statistics report shows 1.6% (sixteen out of one thousand) of children between the ages of 12–17 were victims of rape/sexual assault (page 18).

A study conducted in 1986 found that 63% of women who had suffered sexual abuse by a family member also reported a rape or attempted rape after the age of 14. Recent studies in 2000, 2002, and 2005 have all concluded similar results.

Children who had an experience of rape or attempted rape in their adolescent years were 13.7 times more likely to experience rape or attempted rape in their first year of college.

A child who is the victim of prolonged sexual abuse usually develops low self-esteem, a feeling of worthlessness and an abnormal or distorted view of sex. The child may become withdrawn and mistrustful of adults, and can become suicidal.

Children who do not live with both parents as well as children living in homes marked by parental discord, divorce, or domestic violence, have a higher risk of being sexually abused.

In the vast majority of cases where there is credible evidence that a child has been penetrated, only between 5 and 15% of those children will have genital injuries consistent with sexual abuse.

Child sexual abuse is not solely restricted to physical contact; such abuse could include noncontact abuse, such as exposure, voyeurism, and child pornography.

Compared to those with no history of sexual abuse, young males who were sexually abused were five times more likely to cause teen pregnancy, three times more likely to have multiple sexual partners and two times more likely to have unprotected sex, according to the study published online and in the June print issue of the *Journal of Adolescent Health.*

The message? *God is able to save!*

> The LORD is watching everywhere, keeping
> his eye on both the evil and the good.
>
> —Proverbs 15:3 (NLT)

CHAPTER 3

Ten, a Difficult Age
Part Two: Disobedient
Disaster

It was still in the summer of 1976. We lived in the Lockhart town limits. As mentioned in chapter 1, we were very busy trying to fix up the property. We were blessed with wonderful neighbors that assisted us in the cleaning process.

One of the highlights about the property is a massive oak tree. The tree is right in the center of the lot. Its branches are large and low enough to place a swing. The mighty oak provided a lot of shade from the sunlight. The tree actually gave the property character.

As we were working on clearing some of the prickly vines in the backyard, we spotted an old wire fence. The fence was wrapped with prickly vines, so we made the fence a prerogative.

As we began clearing the fence of the prickly vines, our neighbor, Gloria, yanked on one of the vines. It snapped. The vine whipped through the air, and one of the thorns struck my mother in the eyeball. Everyone heard her screams. We all stopped to see what was wrong. Terrified and panicked, we all saw my mother cupping her face with her hands. Blood was seeping between her fingers, and we knew this was serious. All of us were horrified!

"Mi ojo [my eye]! Mi ojo [my eye]!" my mom screamed.

Our neighbors called my dad Jimmy. "Jimmy! Something is wrong with Maria!" someone yelled. Dad came running.

Dad took my mother to the hospital, and a few hours later, my mom came home with a patch over her eye. We were all afraid that she had lost her eye. We walked my mother in our new home and led her into one of the air-conditioned rooms. She laid down to rest from her terrible ordeal.

Dad wanted us to leave Mom alone and let her rest.

I told my mother that I loved her and that I was going to our neighbor's house, Frank, to play. *To this day*, I remember her saying, "Don't go into the street."

I said, "Okay." At this, I went outside and walked to our neighbor's house to play catch with a baseball.

My neighbors had a chain-link fence surrounding their home. Ms. Mary Dean (Frank's sister) said to me, "Don't you go into the street, Stevie. Yo momma told you not to get into the street."

I answered, "Yes, ma'am." Satisfied at my response, Ms. Mary Dean went inside her house.

As we continued to play catch, Frank threw the baseball over my head and ended up you know where—in the street! Frank was obese and was slow. Frank said, "I'll get it."

In knowing Frank was not as fast as I was, I thought it best that I should get it. Without a second thought, I ran.

I ran to the gate, and just before I could open it, I heard Frank yelling, "No, Stevie! Don't go in the street!"

Too late. I was now through the gate and in the street. I bent down and picked up the baseball. Right then, I saw a car coming directly at me. I literally froze with paralyzing fear! I do remember my mind yelling at my feet, "Rrruuunnn!" My feet didn't listen.

Everything went black. I do not remember how long I was unconscious, but I do remember waking up to sounds slowly coming to my ears. It was the sound of my neighbors yelling and screaming in horror. Their screams were faint at first, and as I gradually was coming to, the sounds became louder. It was then that my eyes slowly began to open. Slowly, I began to notice something I had never experienced. I began to see silhouettes of people standing around.

I was later told that the car had struck my left leg.

The really odd thing was that I saw Gloria crying and cupping her mouth with her hands even though all I noticed of Gloria was her silhouette. I neither saw her facial features nor did I see her hair or her clothing. I knew that it was Gloria because of her voice.

Slowly, everything began to come into view. I do not remember crying, even though the story goes that I was. My head was the only part of my body I remember moving. When I finally was able to fully open my eyes, I realized that I was looking at the license plate of the car. The rest of my body was under the car.

I do not remember much after that. I do remember my mother holding me in the back seat of the car, the patch covering her wounded eye. The people that had struck me were driving us to the hospital. The very hospital where Mom just came from a few hours ago from her terrible eye experience.

Once at the hospital, I remember the doctor taking x-rays of my left leg. There were no signs of any abnormalities or disfigurements. There was only a huge purple bruise on my thigh.

"I want to keep him overnight for observation," the doctor stated.

"No. He is all right," my dad replied. He turned, looked at us, and said, "Come on, let's go home." My dad was not someone you compromised with. His voice projected respect and fear. A construction laborer for over fifteen years and a degree in street smarts, you didn't toy around with Dad. His hands were strong as his mind.

So we left and went home.

A few years went by. A bump was emerging from my left leg.

I became more and more athletic. I was running two to three miles every other day. I was lifting weights. On Saturdays, I was playing football at Memorial Stadium in Austin, Texas. Memorial Stadium is where the Texas Longhorns played college football. At that time, the public was given access to play on the football field.

It was such a rush to run up and down the field. Kicking field goals and actually putting the football through the uprights. All kinds of guys would show up on a Saturday afternoon. Sometimes, we played touch football, and other times we played tackle.

I had no respect for my body when it came to football. I would throw my body all over the field. Many times I came home with rug burns on my arms, knees, legs, and back. Showers showed no mercy on those rug burns. They burned really bad!

In all my athleticism, I never had issues with my left leg other than the *bump* becoming more and more obvious. It was starting to show. Because I ran so much and my legs were very muscular, I chalked it up as muscle.

It got to the point that the bump was now an abnormality. This was not muscle. So I told my mother about it. After looking at it, my mother decided that I needed to have that bump looked at by a doctor. We were referred to a bone specialist in San Marcos, Texas.

William C. Nemeath was my bone specialist in San Marcos. Dr. Nemeath was a big burly guy. Bearded, heavyset, and with a deep voice. Yet he was a very kind man with good bedside manners.

After a few x-rays, they revealed a bone tumor had developed over the course of five years. By this time, the tumor was half the size of a grapefruit. Dr. Nemeath said that the tumor needed to be removed. There was no alternative. We agreed with Dr. Nemeath's assessment, and a date was set.

After surgery, Dr. Nemeath said that he had to saw the tumor off. How did he accomplish this? I can picture me laying on the operating table, my leg filleted open, and him sawing back and forth until the tumor came off the femur. I was astonished in hearing Dr. Nemeath describe the surgical process.

So what happened on that warm summer day? First, I was not given an option; I was given a directive! If Mom had given me that warning in the King James Version, it would have sounded like, "Thou shalt not go into the street! For in the hour that thou goest, a car shall surely run thee over." I was told not once—but twice! Still, I rebelled.

Because I rebelled, I would never play football again. I had to use caution with my left leg. In everything I did, I had to be acutely aware of my leg, especially when it came to physical fitness. Kind of like looking over your shoulder the rest of your life.

In rebelling, I demonstrated the serious price for that rebellion. I had inconvenienced my hurting mother, who needed rest; I involved my neighbors, who thought I was dead; and I involved that innocent driver, who must have thought that he killed me.

One of the most painful lessons I have ever learned came from this experience. Rebellion can cost you your life; and in many cases, it does.

> Children, obey your parents because you belong
> to the Lord, for this is the right thing to do.
> Honor your father and Mother. This is the first
> commandment with a promise: if you honor
> your father and mother, things will go well for
> you, and you will have a long life on the earth.
>
> —Ephesians 6:1–3 (NLT)

CHAPTER 4

Alcoholism

After I became an adult, I remember my dad telling me a story of when I was a young boy. Our parents, on occasions, would take my sister Terri and me to Spanish dances. While I don't recall the age, I do remember laughing with Dad about this one particular moment.

The story goes…

On this certain Saturday night, we had gone to hear one of my parents' favorite Spanish bands. Once the band started playing, a lot of people were dancing and having fun. I remember the dance hall being very hot. There was nothing entertaining for me to do. When I was bored and hot, I had the tendency to "explore."

So when I became thirsty, did I ask my parents for a coke? *No!* Whenever my parents were on the dance floor, I quenched my thirst by sipping on my mom's drink. The initial taste was bitter yet kind of sweet and salty all at the same time. It was *different*. A little interesting. Maybe? The taste called for more investigation.

As the night progressed, I would constantly tell my dad, "Aren't you and Mom gonna go dance?" Little did my dad know why I had posed that question.

"Not right now, *mijo*. We are tired and we need to rest." My mom would then take a drink.

Dad reminded me that not long after that, I was out! He said he couldn't understand why I was so tired. What was really baffling to him is how Mom's drink was full when she left for the dance floor and almost half full when she returned. He said that he and Mom were trying to make sense of it.

Dad said that the next morning when I didn't ask him to go fishing, he knew something was up. Every Sunday, Dad could count on me asking him to go fishing.

The giveaway came when I told Mom, "Mom, my head hurts so bad."

Dad said that Mom responded with a very sarcastic, "Yup, margaritas will do that to you." The jig was up; my secret had been discovered.

The legal drinking age in Texas in 1985 was nineteen years old. Having turned eighteen in 1985, I was so looking forward to 1986. I never used alcohol in high school or any illicit drugs. I guess that was the only reason I had given my dad to be proud of me.

A few months before my nineteenth birthday, Texas enacted a law that increased the drinking age to twenty-one. Are you serious? I have to wait two more years? I guess I'll just have to wait.

At the age of twenty-one, I thought I had hit the big time by working at the IRS Service Center in Austin, Texas, in the REI Department. I was taught how to enter data for eight hours a day. My manager at the time advised me that the goal was to type thirteen keystrokes an hour. I thought she was out of her mind. After a while, I became proficient, typing eight thousand keystrokes an hour. I was rather proud of myself.

This Friday afternoon, I was invited with some of my coworkers to a nightclub in Austin. Even though my birthday was not until the coming Monday, we were celebrating early.

The night started off well. I always remembered movies glamorizing drinking alcohol. I remember ordering my first drink *on the rocks*. Boy, was I sophisticated now. Ordering a mixed drink on the rocks sounded so mature, cool, and aged.

Now my taste in clothing was hideous. I was wearing a white sports coat with white pants, a black undershirt, and black shoes. I thought I was all that and a bag of chips. Mr. GQ, if you will.

As the night drew on, the mixed drinks kept coming. I became "happier." I was enjoying myself listening to music and dancing. As

I consumed more and more alcohol, I became more and more uninhibited. I felt free and careless. This was my first time feeling the numbing effects of alcohol and I liked it.

After all the happy birthdays, shouting, and however many drinks I had, the time came for the party to end. I can say that I do not remember walking in the parking lot to get to my car. I do not remember getting into my car and driving home. This would not be the last time I drove this way.

Monday morning came and I came in to work. Then came the news about what had occurred that Friday night. Everybody was smiling as I could not remember half of the things they told I had said or did. What I do remember is waking up Saturday morning in my bed not knowing how I got there.

Then I met Sandra Evans. Out of respect, Sandra Evans is not her real name. I use this fictitious name to protect the person of whom I am talking about.

She was also a transcriptionist as I was. She worked in the same place and in the same department. Sandra was a tad bit taller than I was, but to me, she had natural beauty. I was enamored by her good looks and laughter. Sandra was a good ole Texas country girl with a lot of smarts to go with her beauty.

Sandra introduced me to country and western music. Had you told me in high school that I would listen to country music, I would have thought you were out of your mind. "You Look So Good in Love" was the first George Strait song I heard that I liked. I thought I was losing it! I was used to listening to Journey, ZZ-Top, Boston, Def-Leppard, Van Halen, and The Scorpions, just to name a few.

After convincing me to wear Wrangler Jeans and Justin Roper boots, it was off to the Sundowner, a country-and-western nightclub in Austin. This is where Sandra taught me how to two-step. Our first night out? Yep; I got so trashed I passed out on the way home. Thank goodness she was driving. After I got the hang of two-stepping, you could not keep me out of country nightclubs. I was hooked!

Sandra and I lasted for a year and a half. We went to many nightclubs in Austin, San Antonio, and Dallas, Texas. We spent many nights at the lake called Pace Bend Park, on the outskirts of Austin in

Spicewood, Texas. Sandra and I went to many rodeos and concerts. Sandra and I differed as far as sports were concerned. She was more into baseball, and I was into football. Irrespective of what we were doing, you could always count on alcohol being readily available.

At this time, my alcohol consumption began to skyrocket. I was noticing that I was drinking every weekend. *It's okay. I can stop anytime I want*, so I thought. *Don't even think like this…you got this. Don't worry about it. You are not an alcoholic. After all, a few drinks do not make you an alcoholic.* After listening to that lie, I didn't give it two thoughts; my drinking increased even more. I was okay.

Sandra's sister, Jessica, had a birthday party. We were all having a good time. Eating, drinking, laughing, and listening to music. I got very drunk. Imagine that! I do not remember how Sandra and I got back to the hotel where we were staying.

The next morning, we woke up, and Sandra was not happy. "Do you remember last night?" she asked.

"I remember we were all jamming to music," I answered.

"That's all you remember?"

"Pretty much," I said.

"Stephen, you picked up my sister and body-slammed her on the floor! Do you remember that?"

"WHAT!" I answered in horror. "I did what?"

"You all were talking about football then wrestling, and the next thing you know, I see you pick up my sister and body-slam her on the floor. You thought it was funny. But my sister was crying because you hurt her. She was so afraid of you that she ran into her bedroom. You went after her to apologize, but that's when you and I came back to the hotel. Had we stayed any longer, her boyfriend would have killed you."

I felt so incredibly stupid. I had now done something in a drunken stupor that injured someone. It wasn't long after this incident that Sandra and I went our own way. She had made many attempts to talk to me about the alcohol, but I ignored her every time.

After Sandra and I broke up, I really began living out the night-life. I was a loose cannon, giving no thought to care or concern for the safety of others. I was raring to go. Weekends would find me at The Midnight Rodeo in San Antonio, about sixty miles away from my home. Since I was now a prolific Texas two-stepper, I never had problems finding dancing partners. A cold longneck beer and a hot woman to dance with—yeah, this was the life!

I was very confident as a dancer. I was even stupid enough to think that drinking made me a better dancer. What I thought was confidence was really arrogance; a real, psychotic idiot.

One Saturday night, I had gone to a country nightclub called Country Down Under in San Antonio. This nightclub was underneath a mall in San Antonio. It was very well designed and laid out. The music was great, the beer was cold, and the women were plenty.

After this particular night, I was so intoxicated I remember having to lean on the bar to keep me from falling. I had a cigarette in my hand and a beer in the other. I remember I was staggering so bad. My faculties were so impaired I don't know how I was able to remain standing; and I still had to drive sixty miles to get home!

Again, I have no idea how I made it home without being stopped by law enforcement or killing myself or someone else. I was that idiot that you hate to see driving behind the wheel on a weekend. I am sure there are more colorful adjectives, but we will use *idiot* for now.

The thought came to me again, *Can you really stop drinking on your own?* Again, I chose to ignore it. I didn't care to hear it; I chose to keep drinking because I wanted to continue the nightlife. I brushed the thought aside. Besides, it took away the degradation I felt from the sexual abuse. When I was drunk, I had no shame, no guilt, no feelings, and no thoughts about that moment at ten years old.

I know! Whenever I feel down, I will just pop open a cold one and bury the shame inside. At some point, it has to go away. I had it all figured out.

During this nine-year period, I cared nothing for God. I believed in him, but I didn't want to stop what I was doing. I was having too much fun and to *go to church* required facing things I did not want to face. I was nowhere close to even considering giving up alcohol.

Alcohol became my god. With alcohol, I felt no pain, no embarrassment, no guilt, and no abandonment. Alcohol made me forget the hurts. I actually was deranged in believing that alcohol was the cure. That alcohol was the answer. At least when I was drunk, I didn't have to feel the hurt, so it must be the answer.

Nothing prior to alcohol had ever helped. Even after receiving Jesus in my heart, I would pray when I was sober. Yet I had no results to show for those prayers. The Lord was ignoring me.

By this time, I really thought that God had no need of me and had no purpose for me. In my way of thinking, I simply didn't matter to God. I was delusional into thinking that God could not help me. I was hopeless, and God had no power to help me. In that case, I might as well go all out!

I began to wonder why no one was inviting me to social gatherings anymore. What is the deal? I was noticing that even my immediate family was reluctant to take me to family outings where alcohol would be present. Here we go again; I was being rejected by my family. Another reason to *tie one on*. It was another excuse to feel sorry for myself and bury myself in alcohol. Never did I consider that, just maybe, it was my alcohol problem that no one wanted to be around. After all, who wants to be around a pathetic loser where he is the center of attention?

Another venomous idea; if my own family rejects me, what in the heck would God have to do with me? The deep cut of rejection had just widened in my heart.

I was so lost, so empty, so alone. No one wanted to be around a drunk—a pathetic, slobbering, and stupid drunk. In my mind, even God would have nothing to do with me.

I didn't want this lifestyle anymore. I decided it was time to stop drinking. There was only one problem—I couldn't! Houston, we have a problem! I had reached a point in my life where I could not stop. Hard as I tried, I could not stop drinking. My best efforts would, at best, go a week to two weeks tops, without a beer.

Then my past came rushing back like a tidal wave. The past nightmares were magnified. The humiliation and degradation, embarrassing my family, the sense of loss of control—all of it engulfed me. So I did the only thing I knew; I turned back to getting drunk to numb the pain.

Look at you. You're such a loser. So pathetic. Your mom abandoned you. Your family doesn't want to be around you. Your friends don't reach out to you. You're an embarrassment to your family and friends. Even God won't help you now.

These thoughts invaded my mind every day.

You are worthless. Your mom and dad were right—you are never going to amount to anything. You are a big mistake. They should have never adopted you! When people look at you, they see Hispanic trash. Your dreams are gone, and hope isn't waiting for you. Hah! Even hope has deserted you. Look around you. Do you see anyone who will vouch for you? Do you see anyone coming to help you? Has anyone made an effort to call you? Does anyone care to know how you are doing? And God? Are you kidding? What makes you think God would waste his time on you? God has more important things to do than to try and save a loser like you!

It is easier to believe a lie than to believe the truth. When lies get thrown in your face over and over again, they eventually become truth. I was devastated. Depressed and devoid of any value. Immediately, my thoughts went to *I am gonna die an alcoholic. I am gonna die knowing that I have failed everyone I loved. I have brought this upon myself, and I have lost hope that I will ever be clean. My God, what have I done?*

In 1996, I was living in Seguin, Texas. I was renting a home without a job. Anytime the landlord came to collect, I would tell some lie to pacify them so that I would not have to pay. My excuse? I wanted the money for alcohol.

One particular Friday night, I got drunk. This Friday night would be different.

I came home from a bar and went in the house. I felt the need to talk to someone.

A few weeks prior, I had someone's phone number to call who were former alcoholics. They were Christian and had a ministry. I called the number from my neighbor's house. I told them what was going on. My voice was so slurred. They said that they would not be able to come out and help me. No amount of pleading would bring them out, so I said "Okay" and hung up the phone.

I returned home. I sat on a pallet I had made on the floor consisting of a mattress and some sheets. I had a deep desire to reach out for help. I was desperate, and my motives were sincere. Then the thought came to me, *Call out to God in prayer. And don't hold back what you need to say.*

I began to think, *I don't know if I can say what is deep inside my heart to a holy God. What else am I going to do? And at this hour, who else will answer my call?"*

I got on my knees, drunk. I began to pray, "God, you are the Creator of heaven and earth and all that is in them. I am so scared of you. I know that with one blast of your nostrils, you can wipe me off the face of the earth as though I never existed." I wish I could express how bad I was shaking inside.

I continued, "I reverence you as all powerful and almighty. I am so terrified, God. But here goes. God, you expect me to have faith in you and yet when I have prayed, you have never helped me get rid of alcohol. I have prayed so many times, and you have not come to help me. How do you expect me to have faith in you if you will not help me? I know you don't make mistakes, but I have messed up so bad, Lord. You said of King David that he was 'a man after your own heart.' David was an adulterer and a murderer. But you forgave him. Noah was a drunk, but you helped him.

"You made me, Lord. Why will you not help me? God, I am not blaming anyone or anything for being an alcoholic. I have done this to myself. I am chemically dependent on alcohol. I want to stop, but I can't! Don't you love me? Lord, if you don't send Jesus tonight and I die, I know that I will bust the gates of hell wide open. I won't make it, God. Please, God, I beg you. Please help me. Again, God, I pray this prayer in fear. I know that you can destroy me as though I was never born, but please don't. Please help me, God, in Jesus's name I pray, amen."

I had completely let go. I held nothing back and prayed with all my heart. Terrified and empty, I laid down on the mattress. My blood vessels felt like icicles as I had remembered what I had just prayed. I hoped that I had prayed respectfully.

For a few minutes I gazed up at the ceiling, hoping that I had not just committed the ultimate sin of defiance against the God of all creation. In sincerity, I meant every word.

I drifted off to sleep.

The next morning came. I got up and went to the bathroom and took a bath. When I finished, I dried off and got my clothes on. I was walking down the hallway when it occurred to me, *I don't have a hangover.* No headache or any other symptom from being drunk a few hours earlier. I was clueless.

I went to Walmart to get some items. I went down an aisle that contained beer and other types of alcohol. I kept on going. After I got what I needed, I paid for the items and went home. I wasn't fazed by the alcohol.

Three months later, I went to Walmart again. Again, I went down the alcohol aisle. This time, I remember pointing to the alcohol and saying, "I'm not scared of you anymore." I kept shopping. When I was done, I paid for my items and went home.

Six months have now passed. Out of nowhere, I thought, *When was the last time I had a craving for alcohol?* I was immediately overwhelmed with joy! It was then that I realized that God had sent Jesus that night I went to him in prayer. It was now that I realized that Jesus himself had delivered me from alcohol! It took me six months to see that Jesus had "immediately stretched forth his hand," caught me, and said, *"O thou of little faith, wherefore didst thou doubt?"*

I was clean. God's timing is perfect because in 1998, Dad had passed away. In between 1996 and 1998, Dad was able to see me get sober. I am sure he had doubts because of how shameless I was. To know that Dad saw me clean meant so much to me.

Twenty-six years have passed, and I have not taken another sip of alcohol since 1996.

I am living proof that miracles do happen. I do not question God's power to save. In twenty-six years, I never craved alcohol again. I never relapsed.

I had trusted God, and h e showed me his results!

> If the Son therefore shall make
> you free, ye shall be free indeed.
>
> —John 8:36 (KJV)

CHAPTER 5

Promiscuity

Merriam-Webster defines *fornication* as "consensual sexual intercourse between two persons not married to each other."

According to the Oxford Lexico website, *promiscuous* is defined as "having or characterized by many transient sexual relationships."

As a young boy, my dad said that when I grew up, I needed to "sow [my] wild oats." Have fun. Venture out. *Get it all out of your system.* That way, when the time comes to marry, you will no longer have the urge to "explore." I understood this behavior to be the beginning of manhood.

Dad was not an avid reader of God's Word. If he had, he might have steered me to 1 Corinthians 6:18, where the apostle Paul says, "FLEE FORNICATION. *Every sin that a man doeth is without the body; but he that committeth fornication sinneth against his own body*" (emphasis mine). Oops, missed that one.

Or how about 1 Corinthians 6:9–10 where Paul says, *"Know ye not that the unrighteous shall not inherit the kingdom of God? Be not deceived:* NEITHER FORNICATORS, *nor idolaters, nor adulterers, nor effeminate, nor abusers of themselves with mankind, Nor thieves, nor covetous, nor drunkards, nor revilers, nor extortioners, shall inherit the kingdom of God"* (emphasis mine). Dad would not have missed the very first item mentioned on Paul's list.

So what does a young boy do? I didn't have the word of God then. I listened to my dad.

Dee (not her real name) and I met at the roller-skating rink in North Austin. I was seventeen years old, and Dee was sixteen. What attracted me to her was her baby-face smile. Her face had the image of a porcelain figurine, smooth and soft. Not to mention she looked very nice in her light-colored blue jeans.

Dee and I met at the concession stand and began to talk. She had a little bit of a lisp; this just added to her charm. Somewhere in our conversations, I was able to get her phone number, and I had made plans to call her during the following week.

After I spoke with Dee on the phone, I asked her if she wanted to go out. She agreed. Plans were made for me to pick her up that summer Saturday night in 1984. Wow, I had just graduated high school in June, and I was about to go on my first date.

Saturday came and I picked Dee up. We drove around Austin for a bit and came to a water bank in front of an apartment complex. We parked.

Dee and I talked for what seemed like ten minutes. We went from conversation to kissing. Things got steamy in the front seat, so we relocated to the back of my mother's station wagon. Yeah, I know, *a station wagon?* This was my first experience having sex.

Dee and I had many good memories. Despite having seen Prince and Sheila E. in concert, our relationship eventually faded away.

Fast-forward now four years later. Twenty-one and now nothing was off-limits. From gentlemen's clubs to nightclubs, I was hitting the nightlife hard in Austin. Neon signs, pool tables, saw dust-laced dance floors, DJ playing great music, cold beer, and oh yeah, *hot* women galore! This would eventually lead to an incredible consequence from which I would not recover.

As I mentioned Sandra Evans in chapter 1, I loved Sandra very much. She and I were faithful to each other, and the moments we shared will always remain. But after she and I went our own way, I always remembered the sense of *freedom* when she left. Like even though I loved her, I wanted to *venture* out.

Single again and back to nightlife. Dallas Night Club, rock and roll nightclub Sneakers, The Sundowner, The Broken Spoke, Midnight Rodeo, and Country Down Under in San Antonio, Mexican bars and nightclubs in Austin, San Antonio, and San Marcus—on and on it goes. The point was clear; I was going after women.

With the passing of each weekend and new nightclubs I visited, it seemed as though I was always *going home* with a different woman. Who would it be this weekend? A blond? A redhead? A brunette? A Hispanic?

To me, with different women came the excitement of discovering their own *uniqueness* in bed. Some were passionate and some not. Some were adventurous and some not. Some preferred the outdoors and some didn't. Every woman was different and had their own ideologies about sex, and I wanted to explore! After all, I was *sowing my wild oats.*

No gala was off-limits.

On one family event, a niece's friend was getting married. My niece introduced me to a friend of hers.

The friend and I were talking about her problems. With a Budweiser in one hand and her hand in the other, we left the venue and went for a ride in my awesome 1979 Pontiac Trans-Am. My niece's friend asked if I could take her to pick up some belongings from a friend's house. I said sure, with a sexual motive in mind.

After we got her belongings, we went to my place. As she was telling me about her recent break up, I was subtly trying to find gaps to sneak in hints of sex. She was telling me how mean her ex was. I would pamper her emotions and told her what she wanted to hear.

As she continued to confide in me about her problems, I would inject sexual hints. Like venom, after a period of time, the venom began to take effect. I really had no thought or concern for her experiences. I wanted to know what she was like in bed.

I approached her and kissed her. She didn't decline the advances. *Gotcha!* I said quietly to myself. And so it was.

This is what living is all about. A lot of women. A lot of brew and a lot of sex. Does it get any better than this?

Or so I thought.

After several years of debauchery, I noticed something odd happening. I noticed that no matter how much I loved someone, my feelings began to fade in a short period of time. I would love the person I was with, but then, as quickly as it came, I would abruptly end the relationship. I didn't love this person anymore.

Instead of paying attention to what was occurring, I chose to ignore the sudden change in feelings. I chalked it up as unimportant.

The promiscuity continued.

Weekend after weekend, month after month, and year after year came opportunity after opportunity. Very seldom did I turn down the chance for sex.

Have fun! Go for it! was the sentiment. *I wonder what she is like. Wow, she looks nice. I bet she has a wild side to her! Those jeans look good on her.*

From boots to bikinis, from heels to halter tops, no pretty woman went unnoticed. I had lost respect for women. I had become that very man I hated.

There is nothing wrong with preference. So what if you prefer sex without the responsibility of marriage? Are you ready for marriage? No? Then don't worry about it. Get out there and do your thing. Life is too short to pass up on some good chances. Take your fill, son. Have at it!

I called myself a Christian. More like a hedonistic whoremonger!

The thought never crossed my mind how thoughtless I was. What I did not only affected the person I indulged with but others that loved this person. This was someone's daughter. This was someone's mother. This was someone's granddaughter. This was someone's best friend. She was someone special to those that love her, and I treated many like sex objects.

Around 2013 or 2014, I got involved in another *serious* relationship. Again, I did love the person. Again, my feelings faded away, and I had no more love for that person. Now, I was concerned, and I was going to search why this was happening.

I had asked the Lord to show me why my feelings were fading like this. It didn't take long to figure out that I was paying the consequence of promiscuity. Having lived an undisciplined and immoral sex life, the fear enveloped me as reality had set in. I had destroyed the ability to ever have another healthy relationship.

If you take a piece of tape, place it on a carpet, and lift it up, it will still have the ability to adhere. But if you keep placing the same piece of tape on the carpet over and over and over again, you will find that the piece of tape has neither the qualities nor the ability to adhere to anything anymore. It has become useless. This is where Stephen got the point!

I now recognized what I had done; I had destroyed the God-given gift of intimacy. I knew that I could not let myself get into another relationship because I knew what would happen. In knowing this, there is no sense in thinking, *Well, if I just try harder next time, things might be different.* I could no longer bring myself to use anyone else as I had done in the past. I knew there was no turning back; this part of my life was gone.

Three failed marriages and now I live every day with the misery of knowing I will never have a healthy relationship.

I will never have kids. I will never see them grow up, graduate high school and possibly college. I will never walk my daughter down the aisle, and I will never be my son's best man. I will never watch a movie with my wife. Our kids will never see us grow old. None of these blessings will ever come to fruition because I chose sensuality over the Savior.

I have been told many times, "It's okay. When you least expect it, you will find someone." No, I won't. I have also heard, "You are being too hard on yourself." That isn't true either.

Discipline is not the enemy of love, and consequence is not a curse.

Love is defined as action. It's not what you say; it's what you do.

Consequence is the direct result when I chose to violate the holy dictates of a righteous and holy God.

Time and time again, I chose to violate his holy ordinance. Because of my insolence, I have lost something so valuable—the ability to have that special someone.

> Be not deceived; God is not mocked: for whatsoever a man soweth, that shall he also reap.
>
> —Galatians 6:7 (KJV)

CHAPTER 6

COVID

I want to preface this chapter by saying that I went through COVID-19 twice; once in 2020 and once in 2021. Due to the severity of COVID-19 (SARS pneumonia) in 2021, there are so many things that I do not remember.

During this process, I was in denial about many things. One of which was that I could not reason in my mind how sick I was. I had never been so sick that I was not able to take care of myself. Catching COVID-19 in 2021 was debilitating physically, psychologically, and emotionally.

I will detail my experience in chronological order as best as I can.

*****

It was a sunny Saturday in February 2020. I was bored and wanted to get out of the house. So I called my friend Willie Mayes. No, not the famous baseball player.

I called Willie and said, "Hey, man, I don't feel like being home. Let's go to Columbia."

"Okay," he answered.

Columbia is a twenty-five-minute drive from Prosperity.

I met Willie at the Town Square in Prosperity. We rode in his Chevy Equinox. We talked about an array of topics plaguing the world today. Since it was a lazy Saturday, we took our time getting to Columbia. I say that because Willie is the kind of driver that even Ms. Daisy would complain about how slow he drives.

Willie and I spent some time in Columbia. We had gone to Dick's Sporting Store. I purchased shoes, shirts, and a pair of sweats. I seriously thought about buying a small Clemson Tigers football helmet for my desk at the police department, but I didn't.

After having some lunch, Willie and I decided to come back home. From the time that we left Columbia to the time Willie dropped me off at my car in Prosperity, I told him, "Hey, man, I don't feel good." I felt a little warm. I got in my car and drove home.

I got my items and went inside. I put everything away and decided I was going to lay down. As I lay on the couch, I felt my forehead. Now I felt like I was on fire.

When the night fell, the situation became worse. I called my chief of police, told him that I was not feeling well, and I was not going to come in the following day. He said he understood.

For the next three days, the only time I got up from bed was to use the bathroom. I didn't eat. I drank fluids to stay hydrated, but that was all. I thought I had a bad case of the flu. COVID-19 had not yet been recognized in our area.

It took three weeks to recover. I had never felt that bad in my entire life. When I had gotten sick, at worst, I would catch a cold or something along those lines. This was horrible.

Eventually, everything went back to normal.

As part of our law enforcement training, we are required to view online training videos from the South Carolina Criminal Justice Academy. In one such video, Newberry County Sheriff Lee Foster was interviewed at the Newberry County Memorial Hospital, as he, too, was recovering from COVID-19. Sheriff Foster caught COVID-19 in early 2021. I remember looking at Sheriff Foster and feeling terrible for him.

God bless him. I would hate to suffer like that, I remember thinking. Sheriff Foster was barely able to speak. He struggled with every word he spoke; but he hung in there and gave his account of the difficulty he was facing. Sheriff Foster encouraged everyone to take precautionary measures to prevent from catching COVID-19 and from transmitting the virus.

Sheriff Foster took a long time to recover. I could not have imagined the terrible process he endured.

The first weekend of September 2021. This was my weekend to work. My schedule dictated that I would work Friday (2:00 p.m. to 2:00 a.m.), Saturday (1:00 p.m. to 1:00 a.m.), and Sunday (1:00 p.m. to 1:00 a.m.). However, it didn't quite turn out that way.

I had fallen asleep on my couch Thursday night, watching a movie. I woke up around midnight, Friday morning, with a fever. I took my temperature, and it was one hundred degrees. Since COVID-19 was now running rampant, I called Chief Wesley Palmore to let him know.

"Get yourself checked out. Take this weekend off and go get tested," Chief said.

"Yes, sir," I replied.

I went to bed and woke up Friday morning. I did not feel as bad as I had the night before. I was hopeful that it was not COVID-19. Maybe, just maybe, it was a small case of the flu.

I went to our local health department in Newberry to get a free COVID-19 examination done. Sunday, the results came back positive for COVID-19.

Doggone it. I caught Covid again! I thought. Well, I had better get prepared for at least a two-week hiatus.

Monday, September 6, 2021 came and I was still running a fever but gradually getting worse. Coughing had now come into the picture. When evening came, I laid down to go to bed. By this time, I was coughing so much I had to sit up to get relief. I tried to lay down again, and again, I had to sit up. Breathing had become an issue as well. I knew I had to get to the hospital.

Should I drive? Should I call a friend? Nah, it was too late to call anyone. I'll call for an EMS truck. I called Newberry Communications (dispatch) and told them what was going on. They said that they would send EMS.

Okay. Eli (my cat) was inside. I took a few items and waited. A short time later, EMS arrived, and I was taken to Newberry County

Memorial Hospital in Newberry, South Carolina. What a way to spend Labor Day.

After a short stint in the ER, I was told I would be staying overnight for observation. I called my sister Terri to let her know what was going on. Her voice crackled as she spoke. It hurt to hear her that way, but I had to let her know.

When Tuesday came, I would have to take a trip to Lovelace Family Medicine in Prosperity, South Carolina. I called Rita Bowles and told her what was going on. Rita was so willing to assist me. Rita had taken time out of her busy schedule to come to the hospital and take me to Prosperity.

A special area in the facility had been prepared for those infected with the virus. I had received four monoclonal antibodies injections. One injection in each arm and one in each leg. The injections had to be administered slowly. A terrible burning came with the injections until the process was completed. Once completed, I was told that I had to remain at this facility for a few hours for observation purposes.

Then came the news! I would not be going home. The physicians had already made plans for me to return to the hospital. They had taken the initiative to have a room ready for me when I arrived at the hospital. So I called Chief Palmore and gave him the updates. Chief Palmore said for me not to worry about anything, just get better.

Poor Rita. All this running around for me. What a sweet soul.

Upon arrival at the hospital ER, the nurse was already waiting for me.

"Thank you," I said to Rita.

"Your welcome, hon," she said.

At this, the nurse and I walked to the first-floor elevators. We got in and the doors closed. We got off on the third floor, the ICU floor. When the nurse and I got out of the elevator, we walked around the left corner of the elevators. We walked a little way down the hall and took another left turn, heading toward the nurse's station.

As we were walking, my breathing became more laborious.

What the heck? I thought. I was getting very weak. I motioned for the nurse to stop so that I could catch my breath.

"Do you need a wheelchair?" the nurse asked.

"No," I replied. "I can make it."

I took a few more steps and stopped. I was no longer able to continue as I was now gasping for air. This was the first time I recognized how sick I was. This would also be the first of many times I would grow accustomed to hearing, "Breathe in your nose and out of your mouth." I really could not believe that I was hunched over, struggling to breathe.

"Yes. Get a wheelchair," I said.

This is where everything gets sketchy.

I remember being wheeled into a room. The room was dark, and the best I can remember is seeing two chairs, one across from the other. I stood up and went to sit on a chair.

Some time had passed, and I don't remember if it was still daylight or evening, but I do remember I had to use the bathroom. I stood up and went to the bathroom. I remember breathing heavily once I got there. I could not believe that the little walk from the chair to the bathroom had taken so much out of me. *I'm just tired from earlier*, I thought as I grabbed the bathroom rails for support.

When I was done, the chair seemed so far away. Thinking I could make it to the chair with no problem, I walked normally and sat down. I was huffing and puffing, trying to catch my breath.

This is stupid, I thought. How can walking a few feet cause someone to be that winded? Even after the signs, I was in denial.

A little later on and a catheter was ordered. This was a good thing. It would certainly be convenient as I would soon discover.

The next thing I recall was being in ICU room no. 7. I now needed oxygen to help me breathe. A thick cannula was in my nose. That thing was so uncomfortable. It felt like a huge rubber Q-tip running underneath my nostrils. I also had an IV line in my arm and a pulse ox on my finger.

When you looked out of my ICU room, all you could see was a red brick wall. I would come to view that wall as a prison wall.

I do not recall how much time had elapsed, but now would come some very trying times.

This is where the beginning of what I call the *domino effect* hysterics began.

By now I was so weak that I could hardly move. I constantly sat beside my hospital bed. I will not forget the first time I adjusted myself in my chair. After I adjusted myself, my oxygen levels dropped dramatically. I panicked.

"Oh my God, I can't breathe! Nurse! Help me, I can't breathe!" I yelled. It was that overwhelming sense of helplessness. I was in horror. The more I tried to breathe, the less air I was taking in. At least that's what it felt like.

Susan Kinard was one of my many nurses. Susan was there when I came in; she was there for my entire stay, and she was there for me when I was transported to Encompass Health in Columbia.

"Hey, hey, hey…calm down. Breathe in your nose and out of your mouth," she said.

"I can't!" I said, almost in tears. Susan saw the horror on my face. As hard as I tried to do as I was instructed, I was too panicked to obey her. I was doing everything but what she said.

"Yes, you can!" she said. "Come on, try to calm down and breathe in your nose and out of your mouth. You can do this. I am right here with you, and I am not going to leave you."

This was also the first time that I was so overcome by fear that I reached out for her hand, still struggling. Susan took my hand and patted my hand, letting me know everything was going to be okay.

I was told that when a person's oxygen level drops below 88 percent, the situation can become dangerous. Dangerous because the person's organs are not getting the necessary oxygen needed for its respective function. This includes the heart, kidneys, liver, and brain. If I remember correctly, I believe my oxygen level was below 80 percent.

Finally, I began calming down. My oxygen levels slowly increased, and I was trying so very hard not to get excited.

"I'm sorry, nurse," I said. "I am sorry. I didn't mean to freak out like that. I just couldn't breathe." Still huffing and puffing. "I have never gone through anything like that before."

"It's okay," she said. "But you can't get excited like that. The only thing that does is make things worse. God is with you and so am I." Susan was very caring, very comforting, and even in her correction, she was so understanding.

I remember one episode in particular. I was going through the domino effect and was panicking again.

"I CAN'T BREATHE!" I yelled.

"YES, YOU CAN!" she replied.

"NO, I CAN'T!" I responded.

"I CAN YELL TOO!" she said. "NOW CALM DOWN AND LOOK AT ME! In your nose and out of your mouth. In your nose and out of your mouth." Susan gave as good as she got. I will always love her for that.

This domino effect caused me to become fearful and anxious. From that moment on, I would do as little as possible so that I would not have to go through that again.

Day after day and night after night, I was imprisoned in the cell of fear and panic. Always careful not to put myself into a position where I would not be able to breathe. It was such a traumatizing experience, and I had realized how important it was to appreciate every breath I take.

Almost the entire time I was in the hospital, I ate as little as possible. This was due to fear of going through the domino effect. My breakfast would consist of Jell-O, very little pudding, Sprite Zero, water, and on occasion, a bite of some actual food. *That's it!* The less I ate, the less I would struggle with going to the bathroom. If I had to use the bathroom, this meant I would have to get up; my oxygen levels would drop, I would begin coughing, which would bring on the domino effect. So the less I ate, the better off I would be. I was that afraid.

Morning after morning, blood was drawn. One morning it would be from my right arm, and the next morning, it would be my left.

Every morning, noon, and night came the breathing treatments. Time after time, I was slowly feeling the effects of the steroids. I was becoming more and more jittery and shaky. I could be in a deep sleep, and out of nowhere, I would suddenly wake up, eyes wide open and extremely tired, knowing I could have slept a little longer. Sometimes out of the blue, I would have uncontrollable jerking motions. To me, it was the equivalent of drinking five cups of coffee and three espresso shots in one hour.

Then, there were times when the hospital bed looked so good. Because of the consistent drop in oxygen, I made it a point to sleep on the chair next to the bed. When I did decide to sleep on the bed, it was a grueling task getting from the chair to the bed. It seemed like it always took at least five to ten minutes to accomplish the goal. I always let the nurse know not to get my oxygen tubes and other wiring crossed in the process of getting to the bed. I wanted the process to be one smooth motion. The less movement the better.

There were times when I thought about how easily I took for granted merely walking to the bathroom. Mentally, there was no way I could accomplish this on my own. The bathroom was only twenty feet away; now it seemed like a mile. I neither had the strength nor the breath to get there. I knew that to try this on my own would have bad results.

I spent my waking hours looking at the clock, wondering what day it was and whether my condition was improving.

When am I getting out of here? Or will I ever *leave?* I feared.

Little by little, I was becoming more and more frustrated as I had no idea what my condition was. How bad are my lungs? Are they saturated with pneumonia? How long will this process take? Do I have permanent damage? I had no information. *Nothing!* No one was talking to me. When I would ask, I got the typical, "It's gonna take time. You are very sick. Your recovery isn't going to come over night." Although it was true, all I wanted to know was how bad of shape I am in.

Some mornings I would wake up using profanity. So frustrated, so fearful. Feeling imprisoned by my condition and not being out there in the world, I would say things I had no business saying. Exhausted and tired from being sick and afraid, colorful words would come flying out of my mouth with impunity. This was very uncharacteristic of me. Feeling ashamed and knowing I had no excuse, I begged God for his forgiveness.

In some of those moments when I could not breathe, I would call out to Jesus, "Please, Lord, give me my next breath. Please, Jesus, you are my hope…I desperately need you right now. I am so afraid, Lord. I am so afraid, Holy Spirit. God of all creation, please give me the privilege of another breath." Many times I would fall asleep with his name on my lips. Afraid, but knowing I was not alone.

I was in ICU for approximately one month. Then, I was told I had my own private room. This was awesome. However, my troubles, by no means, were over.

The standard vitals were taken every day. The one thing I did not realize is that the pulse ox on my finger was somehow connected to the nurse's station. If my oxygen levels dropped below a certain percentage, the nurses knew about it and would check on me to make sure I was okay. They wanted to know why the levels had dropped so drastically. It seemed as though with any little movement, my levels dropped.

I dreaded the mornings the nurses came in to weigh me. I had to get up, step onto the scale, and stand on the scale until it displayed my weight. It never failed; by the time I sat back down on the chair, I was trying hard not to put myself in a breathing frenzy. Over and over again I heard, "Come on, breathe in your nose and out of your mouth," as the nurses tried to help me increase my oxygen levels to an adequate level.

Being in a very weak condition, modesty went out the window. I was not able to clean myself. Initially I was very embarrassed. Who wants to go through something like that? I was humbled through this trying process. While I understood that's what the nurses are there for, it took this drastic measure for me to appreciate them for all that they go through and what they endure.

I was now taking thirteen to fifteen different medications. Every morning around 5:30 or 6:00, the phlebotomist would come in to get blood. I must say, I was blessed with having some great phlebotomists. Almost every time it was a painless process. My breathing treatments, like in ICU, were done three times a day, which still included steroids.

I eventually got to a point that I could no longer cope with the steroids. I told my respiratory nurse, Erica Rickard, the symptoms. I told her I was having a hard time taking them. She told she would speak to the doctor and would let me know.

It was not long after that, that she advised me that the doctor was going to try another nebulizer. It worked great! I no longer suffered the effects of the harsh steroids, and I was so appreciative for what she had done for me.

Erica is a wonderful respiratory nurse. During my stay, I always prayed that I never said anything out of the way mean to her. I feared that through one of my *moments*, I might have said something ugly or not nice to her. I never wanted anything nasty flying out of my mouth.

Erica was given orders to gradually reduce my oxygen levels. Although I do not remember where my oxygen levels were when the process began, I do remember going from 10 percent down to 8 percent. From 8 percent to 6 percent. The process continued until I reached 2 percent. *Trust me*, this was not easy. Again, there was that dread of having to go through the panic phase of not being able to breathe.

I would always ask the nurses if they could increase the oxygen levels when I had to use the bathroom. They were generous and kind enough to oblige. When they turned up the oxygen, I felt a strong flow going through my nose and into my lungs. It felt so good to breathe. This was a reminder to me that I do not have the right to breathe, but it is a privilege coming from God to have the next breath.

Erica had to be firm, but she was not going to let me remain weak just because I was afraid. She was persistent and yet caring enough to help me through it. I always tried to be kind and considerate.

On one occasion, I asked a nurse, "Why am I so weak? Why can't I just get over this?"

"You almost died," she said. "The doctors wanted to put you on a ventilator. I asked them to give you one more hour. You were that close."

Death? Me? Now? I thought. How many others paid the ultimate price at the hands of COVID-19? Countless. This was one of those epiphanies when I realized how close to death I was. Just when I thought it couldn't happen to me, I was that close to meeting the Lord.

As time passed, I had physical therapists come in to get me to walk again. It seemed like they always showed up around 11:00 a.m. To my disgrace and shame, I didn't try as hard as I should have. Goodness, I cannot say "I'm sorry" enough for wasting their time. They did try hard to help me.

"Not today," I once replied.

Without missing a beat, Erica said, "Document it." She wasn't mean, but she was there to let me know "I'm not putting up with your childishness." Tough cookie! I appreciated that about her.

Then came walking. I still recall some of the steps I actually took; it had to be with a walker. First, five steps and back. Then as I got stronger, it was ten and back. Eventually, I would walk to the door and back.

How bad was I off? To give you an idea, the first time I walked in the hallway (with the walker) with the nurses beside me, the nurses were clapping, as were those in the nurse's station. I would have to stop to catch my breath and then I would continue. Then I would make my way back to my room, sit down, and struggle to regain normalcy in my breathing.

The feeling was indescribable. To have the nurse staff cheering me on was a powerful motivator; I had made someone proud.

Sometimes, it was short-lived.

The next day, I would be so exhausted from the walk in the hallway. Again, I would use the workout as an excuse not to continue with physical therapy the next morning.

Again, I became angry and frustrated. I wanted to go home. I still didn't have any news about the condition of my lungs.

I'm not doing anything else! I whined mentally. Pouting like a pathetic, immature child. Thank goodness God knows how to build bridges to get over the Whine River.

I was also assigned an occupational therapist. She was fantastic. Like Erica, she was firm and unwilling to let me take the easy road.

I had to work for everything. I had to learn to brush my teeth again. When I sat up, she would push the water basin away from me; I had to stand up and reach for it. I would brush my teeth standing up and when I was finished, my reward was to sit down. Again, I had to hear, "Breathe in your nose and out of your mouth."

I had to give myself a sponge bath. She would push the basin away from me. I had to reach for it. I would soak the cloth in warm water. The first time I felt warm water on my funky self, it was incredible! Very exhilarating! Calgon had nothing on this!

You have to keep in mind, I had not bathed since the day I was admitted in the hospital. Actually, my last shower was that Thursday morning before catching COVID-19 in September.

Everywhere I washed was a task, but it was worth it. Everything she asked me to do required effort; nothing came easy.

I was assigned a case manager, Rebecca Clary. She was a consistent care provider, making sure I was doing okay. Although I do not recall the time lapse, Rebecca came to my room one day to tell me I would soon be released to go home.

Well, I was going to get what I wanted—to go home! There was only one problem; I still couldn't walk. Now I realized how stupid I had been. I was still not able to fend for myself, and to make matters worse, I live alone. What am I going to do? I cannot get around on my own. I can't even shower here without nurses present. What in the world makes me think I am going to shower by myself? Reality flooded my mind: *You're an idiot!*

"Rebecca, I can't walk," I stated with a panicked overtone.

"Let me see what I can do," she said.

I believe it was the following day that Rebecca came in and offered me some options.

"I found a place in Greenville called ATI, or there is Encompass Health in Columbia. Both facilities specialize in acute physical therapy rehab," she said.

"I will do anything," I said, knowing how dumb I had been. I had realized the desperation I was in.

"Well, here is some information on both places. Do a little research and let me know which one you would prefer."

"Okay," I said.

I chose Encompass Health in Columbia.

Three days later, I was transported to Columbia via EMS.

Since I was admitted to Encompass Health, the staff was excellent. Nurses, therapists, home keeping; if anyone had a bad day, I never saw it. Always smiling, jovial, outgoing, very knowledgeable, and caring.

I spent twelve days at Encompass Health with a totally different attitude. My demeanor and my countenance had changed. I knew I was going to have to work really hard and give 110 percent effort into therapy. Failure was not an option. I chose to succeed.

I truly believe that the Lord's inspiration had elevated me to an incredible level. Every day I looked forward to working out, walking, lifting light weights, and giving it everything I could muster. If another patient opted out of therapy, I was not only willing but excited to take their place.

My therapy sessions were scheduled with precision. Monday through Sunday, the doctors, nurses, and therapists were always on time. The doctors came in every morning to check on me to review progress and to make sure I was okay and if I needed anything.

The food at the facility was delicious. I marveled at how good it was. They were very well organized in scheduling the meals of the day.

Time and time again, Rita Bowles would wash my clothes and make the journey from Pomaria, South Carolina to Encompass Health, thirty miles away.

Rita and I laughed at one funny incident. I had lost a considerable amount of weight. I was using a pair of Hal's (Rita's husband) shorts. During a therapy session in the gym, I was speaking with my therapist when all of a sudden, my shorts dropped down to my ankles. Ooops! I looked around as eyes were honed in on my folly and my fruit of the looms. Talk about deer in the headlights look!

Sharonda Chaffins, my pastor's wife, brought homemade fried chicken, rice, and my favorite, green bean casserole with brown sugar and bacon. *Sharonda can cook! Like OMG!* Absolutely delicious!

There were times when I would get on the wheelchair and venture out of my room just to get out and explore. I also was trying to get my strength back. The staff allowed me to do this, but there were certain areas I was prohibited from going; precautionary measures.

By now, I was able to take showers on my own, use the bathroom, brush my teeth, get in and out of bed on my own, and all the other basics of taking care of myself. I was walking regularly, though not far. I knew the day was drawing near. I was excited.

Gone was the attitude of pity. Gone was the anger. Gone was waking up using profanity. Gone was the frustration. Gone was the paranoia. Pity, anger, profanity, frustration, and paranoia had been replaced with enthusiasm, inspiration, dedication, motivation, and a mind made up to succeed. I had determined to be joyful in the pain and to be thankful in the failures.

On the ninth day at Encompass Health, I was told I would be leaving in three days. I felt stronger. I felt more alive. More and more color was coming back. It was the first time in a long time that I felt good. I was going to miss everybody at Encompass Health.

My pastor, James Chaffins, came and picked me up on my scheduled release date. All my belongings had been packed, and I was ready to leave.

We got into his Ford pickup, put all my stuff in his truck, and off we went; I was actually on my way home. The air was so fresh. The sky seemed brighter and more vibrant. Everything around me seemed so sharp with contrast, color, and clarity. Sounds were so clear and crisp. It felt so good to be alive! God had given me another chance; God had walked with me through another major storm.

I was home! This was the first time since the first week of September that I had entered my home. When I was alone, I took a moment and just enjoyed the quiet as I sat on my couch. Just me and my oxygen.

"Thank you, God. I am home *only* because of you. All praise and honor are yours. Thank you, God, for saving me. Thank you, God!"

Although I still had a tough road ahead of me, I knew I was out of death's grip; God had done it again as only he can!

November 22, 2021, I was allowed by my doctor to return to work on light duty status. Every day was a struggle going through the process of getting up and going to work, but I was so thankful to have gotten this far.

You cannot imagine how wonderful it felt to drive again. To be back in the world again. To breathe again. Now the words *breath* and *breathe* have so much value. Anytime I hear those words, I am very sensitive in understanding not to take it for granted.

When I returned, I was overwhelmed with kind words and many hugs. It seemed everywhere I went, I was greeted with "Good to see you back" and "It's so good to see you in uniform again." Everyone from my guys at the Prosperity Police Department to Prosperity Town Council, The Blend (coffee shop), Carter Lake of State Farm Insurance, and Dianna Naczi of Dianna Lynne Design. I was amazed at the heartwarming reception I had received.

Darian Morris, assistant manager at Food Lion, said, "If you need something, let me know. We got your back."

Sheena Paige said, "Oh my God, you're back! It's so good to hear from you again." While I was at the hospital, Sheena had sent me flowers in an angel vase, with a card to let me know she cared. The comment was simple, but the concern and care was valuable to me.

I received warm hugs from Jordan Barnes, who was also one of my nurses. Many times, I would see Jordan at the hospital. She was very attentive to my needs; wonderful bedside manners and a beautiful heart, a sweet spirit with an angel face. Jordan is a *great* nurse!

After many visits to my physician, Dr. Edwina Hallman, I was released to full duty status on January 20, 2022. By this time, I was still taking ten to twelve medicines a day, on nebulizer treatments, and of course, still on oxygen.

Even though I was getting better, I didn't realize the impact COVID-19 had on memory loss.

I was speaking with Newberry County Deputies Devin Kingsmore and Wesley Blackburn. They reminded me that they came to see me at the hospital. Initially, I didn't remember the visit.

"Yeah, brother, Blackburn and I asked the nurses if we could see you, and they said yes. I came into your room, and you were out. I tickled your feet, and you woke up. We had a conversation with you. You don't remember that?"

"Not really," I said.

"We didn't stay long. We just wanted to come see you and check on you." Devin and Wesley had official business at the hospital and made it a point to check on my condition.

I remember James Chaffins and Rita Bowles coming into my room, but I do not remember what we talked about. I was more concerned about saying something wrong or out of the way because I was frustrated at not being able to breathe.

My case manager, Rebecca Clary, had come to check on me. Like before, I could not remember what we had talked about. I felt awful because Rebecca is a wonderful case manager, and it saddens me that I didn't remember. It's almost like someone took probes, put them in my head, and erased many of the things I did and conversations I had.

One hour. I was that close to death. One hour.

He brought me up also out of an horrible pit, out of the miry clay, and set my feet upon a rock, and established my goings.

—Psalm 40:2 (KJV)

CHAPTER 7

Consequences

Adoption

To the best of my knowledge, I was told I was adopted when I was fourteen years old. I didn't feel that it had affected me in a negative way. I accepted things the way they were; my parents were Santiago and Maria Selestino.

I was a pretty normal kid in Lockhart, Texas. Always riding my bike, running around with my pup Tuffy, hanging out with my cousins, and watching movies at the old Baker Theater.

There were many outings with family. Vacations. Trips to the San Antonio Zoo. Aquarium visits in Corpus Christi, Texas. Carnivals, parades, and the annual Lockhart Chisholm Trail Round-Up were just a few family events we shared.

As I grew older, I began to think more about my biological mother. What does she look like? Is she married? Does she think about me? Why did she give me up? Do I have any biological brothers and sisters? These questions ran through my head over and over again. I was too afraid to ask my mom about the adoption for fear that I would hurt her.

I confided in my sister Terri. She told me that my sister was shouting for the Selestino family not to take me away. From the way Terri described it, my biological sister was devastated.

I became angry at Delia. I carried the anger for so many years. I had no evidence to refute my assumptions that Delia had abandoned me. It took years to accept what I was told as fact: Delia was not able to financially feed another mouth.

Eventually, through years of mental and emotional struggles, I had come to the realization that Delia did her best. I had come to understand that Delia did not reject me; I had placed blame on someone who didn't deserve it.

The consequences for being angry for all the wrong reasons and for so many years had allowed myself to become a miserable person. I was always angry about something, *especially* when I was drunk. During my drunk stage, I always thought that I was a nice guy. I was so wrong!

Anger is only one letter away from danger!

Sexual assault

The sexual assault that was inflicted on that ten-year-old boy in the creek that day was devastating. There was no rhyme or reason as to why it took place, but it happened. I had always vowed in my heart that I would never forgive this individual.

As time passed, my hate grew deeper and more profound. When I was very athletic, lifting weights, running three to four miles every other day, and doing martial arts, I wanted to snap his neck. I wanted him to suffer tremendously as I had suffered. I wanted to see fear in his eyes as I stood over him, ready to stomp on his throat. I had absolutely no mercy, and if I had seen him, I certainly would not have thought twice in sending him to the hospital. I was fueled with hatred and blinded by vengeance. I even went so far as to think I could end his life. I was that angry.

This unhealthy anger appeared in so many other areas in my life. This was the hardest roller coaster ride I had taken. If a certain person looked a certain way, "I hate him." If someone said something I didn't agree with, "I hate her." If a group had a different worldview, "I hate them." I didn't know how to express the deep-rooted anger, resentment, bitterness, and hostility. I only knew anger.

Did I have any reason to be angry? Yes. But that reason was unwarranted when I had directed the anger at someone who was not the violator. I was angry and rightfully so, but I had no right to smear it on anyone else's life.

For all my excuses, there was never any rest. For all my complaints, there were never any satisfying answers. For all the people I vented to, I was still empty. What the heck was I missing? I don't get it! Will someone please tell me!

Even after I had received Christ Jesus as my Savior, there was no getting away from the rage. Not until I read the words of Jesus, *"If you forgive those who sin against you, your heavenly Father will forgive you. But if you refuse to forgive others, your Father will not forgive your sins"* (Matthew 6:14–15 NLT).

Wait…what? You mean to tell me I have to forgive that pervert? Seriously? I am having to cope with the emotional roller coasters through the various stages of my life for something I didn't do. I was the one who was wronged. I was the one who was humiliated. I was the one who was violated. I was the one who was degraded. And you're telling me I HAVE TO FORGIVE HIM?

Okay, so because I was assaulted, I am right, and God is wrong? Jesus never said, "Unless, you are sexually abused, you are to forgive. If you have been sexually abused, you do not have to forgive." Jesus clearly said, *"But if you refuse to forgive others, your Father will not forgive your sins."* God didn't mince words! God is holy. I am not!

When I relented and asked God to help me forgive, I was on the road to healing. There is more power in forgiveness than there is to seek someone's demise. This process would take years to reach spiritual maturity.

I have come to know that anger has played a big part in my life. Today, I still struggle with acceptance and some emotional imbalance. The difference is God has allowed me to see the coming storms. Just as a bright and sunny day gives way to thunderstorm clouds, so I am now able to see a storm coming. Though the appearance of the storm may be ominous and frightening, God has given me the maturity and boldness to say, "Okay, Lord, I see it coming. Please help in the midst of what I am about to face. Jesus, walk on the sea of my imperfectness and weakness. According to your will, calm the storms at your biding, for I will not survive it without you. Take my hand as I reach for you, and get me through it, Lord. In Jesus's name, amen."

The sexual abuse was not my fault. Because of what happened, I know I will always struggle internally. Just as Jesus forgave me, so I chose to forgive him and left the results to God. May God be merciful to him.

Rebellion

How does God view rebellion? First Samuel 15:23 (KJV) says, "For rebellion is as the sin of *witchcraft*, and stubbornness is as iniquity and idolatry" (emphasis mine).

Witchcraft is the Hebrew word *qesem* [keh'-sem] which means divination. Divination means to be consulting familiar spirits. It is the same as consulting a medium, fortune-teller, or soothsayer. Translated: consulting demons.

My parents have a God-given authority to exercise rule over my sister and me. At ten years old, I was not asked if I wanted to obey my parents; I was told to. When I disobeyed my parents, I violated God's sacred command to honor my mother and my dad. Even my friend Frank, who was older than me, gave me a directive. Since I was with him that day, he now had the rule over me.

When I ran out of that gate, I was in complete rebellion; I was being an imp. The end result was that I was injured. Years later, I would have surgery to have a bone tumor removed. Now, for the rest of my life, I bear the scar of that rebellion. Had that car been traveling any faster, I would have been crushed underneath that car. My family would have been devastated, and the driver of that car would have to carry the mental burden of having killed a child.

God authorized Adam not to eat from the tree of the knowledge of good and evil. In the day that he did eat of it, *"thou shalt surely die"* (Genesis 2:17; emphasis mine). In Genesis 3:4, the serpent told Eve, "Ye shall not surely die." Both disobeyed God and the consequences followed immediately.

Same principle. Same correlation. Same result. When I rebelled, I chose to listen to demons. "It's okay…go get the ball, you will not get hit by that car." That advice sounds familiar, doesn't it? Guess what? The same spirit that lied to Eve lied to me also. Next thing I know, I was waking up, staring directly at the license plate of the car that had just injured me.

Alcohol

When I abused alcohol, I was acting out my aggression and pain. I thought alcohol provided two things I desperately wanted—healing and inhibition.

Healing because when I had consumed enough alcohol, I was *numb*. My emotions were numbed, and it gave me a false sense of security; I was safe from the past. The more I drank, the less I felt. I never saw that *more* would one day take me down a road of recklessness and destruction.

After a while, the numbness had no more power. In my drunkenness, my past was coming back with greater magnification. Alcohol was magnifying my pain. So I drank more and more. I wanted that lie. That lie that said that alcohol was the answer to my past. By this point, I was beyond help.

Inhibition because I had freedom. I was so mindless and ignorant in thinking that freedom was *letting it all hang out*. Live out my fantasies; just live it up! Be careless and throw caution to the wind! Have fun, you only live once…do it, do it!

Alcohol reveals the nudity of the soul and mind, and I was naked. Naked in the sense that I was without dignity and shame. I had no sense of decency, character, or class. I was out of control.

I didn't care who got hurt so long as I got what I needed or what I thought I needed. Despite the risks, I took stupid chances driving drunk. I didn't think of an officer going to my home to tell my loved ones I was killed in a car accident and the contributing factor was alcohol.

The thought never crossed my mind that someone's mother, pregnant sister, little child, someone who just graduated high school or college, a dad who just got that long-awaited promotion, the retired couple who was traveling, or even you—the thought never came to me that I could have killed one of these precious people.

Seguin, Texas was my finish line. I was exhausted. I had finally come to my Red Sea. I didn't have Moses or Aaron. I didn't have Joshua. God had allowed me to do all this running around, but now the time had come to stop…just me and God.

What are you going to do, Stephen? You can't go back to Egypt. Take a good look at your Red Sea. You don't have a boat. You don't have a raft. What are you going to do?

I dropped to my knees and said, "I give up, God. Here I am, a sloppy drunk. I have been running for too long. I am undone. I am at my end. I realize if Jesus doesn't help me, I will drown. I can't do this anymore, and I don't want this anymore. Will you please help me?"

God parted the Red Sea!

Even though I live with a lot of regret, God has touched me in such a way that I have never touched another drop of alcohol since 1996. Nor have I craved alcohol.

I celebrate my God and boast of his mighty power. My Savior made a way where there was no way. By the grace of God, I am here today to speak of God's great mercy: mercy that I *do not* deserve!

My God is able!

Promiscuity

This is a very delicate area to touch on. This is something I am not proud of; rather, I am ashamed that I ventured down this path and hurt many people along the way.

I bragged about how much I enjoyed living this lifestyle; now, it is a disgrace and a shameful reminder of my once-debauched life. I am embarrassed to reflect back and see an awful man using women as a means to try to find acceptance and worth. To me, if a woman accepted my advances, then I was, at the very least, worth sleeping with. I had some type of value.

I was minimizing the importance of women. Women are not rungs on ladders for the purpose of attaining self-worth; they have intrinsic value. Jesus himself said it this way, *"For husbands, this means love your wives, just as Christ loved the church. He gave up his life for her*" (Ephesians 5:25 NLT). God views women as having such incredible importance that men are commanded, not requested, to love them and give up their lives for them.

> Know ye not that ye are the temple of God, and that the Spirit of God dwelleth in you? If any man defile the temple of God, him shall God destroy; for the temple of God his holy, which temple ye are. (1 Corinthians 3:16–17 KJV)

> What? Know ye not that your body is the temple of the Holy Ghost which is in you, which ye have of God, and ye are not your own? For ye are bought with a price: therefore glorify God in your body, and in your spirit, which are God's. (1 Corinthians 6:19–20 KJV)

Fornication is a sex violation against God's standards. Sex is *only* blessed by God in the marital bedroom. What rebuttal can anyone bring against God's word? Whenever someone says to me either "You are quoting that out of context" or they think I am not understanding, I simply end the conversation quickly and walk away. There is no sense in arguing a topic where someone feels for me and wants me to be happy with someone versus God's word! I honestly do appreciate their thoughts and prayers; but "thy Word is truth" (John 17:17).

I stand firm on Paul's preaching in the two passages in 1 Corinthians and Ephesians. If you violate the speeding laws, you get a ticket. If you break the law, you go to jail. Just because someone has sympathy for you doesn't mean you are going to get out of or get away with the violation. I cannot turn from what is true; and what I have done has had consequences that will remain.

I know that God can heal without a doubt. God is able. I know without a doubt that God loves me and has forgiven me. However, I also know that I suffer consequences because of my direct disobedience (rebellion) and violation against a holy God.

COVID

When my dad was suffering through chronic asthma, it always hurt to see him struggling to breathe. Here I was, twenty-five years later, gasping for air myself. I cannot fathom going through this year in and year out as Dad did. I don't mean this in a harsh way, but I am glad Dad was not around to have suffered through this virus.

I am more cautious now when I am out and about. I move slower. I walk slower. Always paying attention to my lungs when I start breathing heavily. I still use oxygen at night, just to give my lungs a break. I have come to the conclusion that I have sustained permanent lung damage as a result of the SARS pneumonia.

It saddens me to know that so many people lost loved ones to this dreaded virus. I lost a cousin in Michigan because of COVID-19.

All over the world, people are in mourning. Could this virus have been prevented? Were there more steps that could have been taken to protect our families and loved ones? I think that we, and the medical professionals, did the best we could with the information we had.

We know the horrors of suffering through COVID-19. I pray for God's will in this circumstance, both here and all over the world. My condolences for all who have lost their special loved ones; may the love of God, his Christ, and his Holy Spirit embrace you in your hour of need and healing.

In the end, God will be honored and glorified.

O the depth of the riches both of
the wisdom and knowledge of God!
How unsearchable are his judgments,
and his ways past finding out!

—Romans 11:33 (KJV)

CHAPTER 8

His Story

In Genesis 22, God tells Abraham to take his only son Isaac, whom Abraham loved, to the land of Moriah. Once there, Abraham is to build an altar and offer Isaac as a sacrifice. Abraham did as God said.

Abraham built the altar, laid the wood in order, bound Isaac, then laid him on the altar on the wood. Abraham then took a knife and just as he was about to slay Isaac, I'm paraphrasing, the Angel of the Lord told Abraham to stop. God saw Abraham's heart. Isaac was spared and the knife stopped.

Fast-forward.

On that same mountain, God offered his only beloved Son, Jesus Christ, as the perfect sacrifice for all. Only this time, the knife was not stopped. The knife pierced the heart of Christ, and he died.

This is the greatest act of God's love ever demonstrated.

Why did God do that? I believe God did this for two reasons. First, love has to be proven and second, for the hope of eternal life with him in heaven.

Love has to be proven. Abraham proved his love to God by his willingness to offer up Isaac, his only beloved son. I cannot fathom what Abraham must have been going through. I am sure that he was overwhelmed with grief, knowing what he was about to do. It was Abraham's faith that overcame his feelings as he was about to plunge the knife in the heart of Isaac.

God proved his love to the world by offering up his only beloved Son, Jesus Christ. Unlike Isaac, the knife was not stayed, and Jesus was not spared. This is the Gospel; that because of your sins and mine, the perfect Son of Yahweh was given on a tree as proof of God's undying, unfading, and everlasting love for us.

In Romans 5:8, Paul reminds us, "But God commendeth his love toward us, in that, while we were yet sinners, Christ died for us."

David Guzik Bible commentary says:

> The work of Jesus on the cross for us is God's ultimate proof of His love for you. He may give additional proof, but He can give no greater proof. If the cross is the ultimate demonstration of God's love, it is also the ultimate demonstration of man's hatred. It also proves that the height of man's hatred can't defeat the height of God's love.

The hope of eternal life with Christ is the purpose of the Gospel.

One of the reasons I have spent so many years in torment is because mentally, there was no way I could ever repay for all those that I have hurt.

Three failed marriages. A life of debauchery and perverseness. A life of hatred, anger, and vengeance. Rebellious. Alcoholic. Financially ruined. Running from my problems. A life all messed up and torn to shreds; pathetic and alone. All of it has come to this point in my life.

All the guilt, all the frustrations, all the bitter losses and disappointments; these accounts I relived again in this book. I cannot begin to tell you the times I have spent on my knees asking God to forgive me for some of the most terrible things I did.

Today, I have no reason to be incarcerated by guilt; I am forgiven! God has been very merciful to me. Every day I am reminded the reason for celebrating every breath my LORD gives me. Every beat of my heart, every step I take, every time I see the blue sky, every time the rains fall, a starry night, a cold and clear night, the sound of ocean waves crashing, the innocence of children laughing and playing. Even when things don't go my way, God is always in the forefront and *never* in the background.

I have no regrets in writing this book. It has been both a challenge and a blessing. This book has taken a lot out of me, but for all the right reasons. Some answers came through going back.

As you have read how terrible and vile a person I used to be, it's a wonder I still have breath. Having contemplated suicide, driving intoxicated, struck by a car, and COVID-19 are just a few of the times I could have died.

I still face the challenges of what happened at ten. Now, when I face emotional challenges, I have God to turn to. He is steadfast and strong, mighty in power, knowing all things. It is him that gets me through every imbalance and inner conflict. He is not the author of confusion, but he is the author and finisher of my faith. I know he is walking with me and beside me every step of the way. When my testing is done, I come out on the other side, my hand in his, because I know God is there!

I still face the challenges of going through COVID-19. I have come to terms in knowing I, more than likely, have sustained permanent lung damage. I am not afraid anymore.

I willingly go through this process because I know that someone out there is hurting far worse than I am. I am privileged to have a godly testimony that understands what that *someone* is suffering through.

This story is about the grace of God. It's about grace sending Jesus to come down to be betrayed, bludgeoned with the cat-o'-nine-tails, and crucified in my place. It was because I owed a debt I could not repay; and here was the Son of God paying my debt he didn't owe.

This story is not about Stephen Selestino; this story is about God demonstrating his love, power, patience, grace, and mercy to someone who didn't deserve it.

Are you facing a raging storm? Do you find yourself in the middle of a violent sea? Are you addicted to something? Are you walking in fear? Are you confused? Are you mentally or emotionally tormented? Have you done something that you feel you cannot be forgiven for? There is hope; there is help, and there is healing for you. You are not outside of God's reach!

Whether you were sexually abused, whether you're an alcoholic, whether you are rebellious and/or promiscuous, I know how you feel; I was there. I have offered my exposed life to God that you, the reader, will not be afraid and know that you can trust God.

So listen deeply when I say you have intrinsic value. You were created in the image and likeness of God himself (Genesis 1:27). You are in God's thoughts and heart, always (Psalm 139:17–18). God has purpose for you (Jeremiah 1:5). Nothing stands in the way of God's love for you (Romans 8:38–39). God's great desire is for you to be eternally with him (John 3:16).

Seek God and allow him to come into your life. God will lead you by his will through the pain, through the tears, through the emptiness, through the darkness, and through the way where there is no way. Take it from someone who should be dead.

> Peace I leave with you, my peace I give unto you:
> not as the world giveth, give I unto you. Let not
> your heart be troubled, neither let it be afraid.

—Jesus

ACKNOWLEDGMENTS

Very Special People

To my family in Lockhart, Texas

- Mom—Maria Selestino
- Sister—Terri Mireles
- Nephews—Albert Gonzales, Jose Lopez, and Julian Mireles
- Brother—Carey and Yvette Manning and family

My family, you are my heart and I love each and every one of you. Thank you for your prayers and for never giving up on God. It was God who, by his divine mercy and will, allowed me to continue on. I have no doubt that God heard your prayers. He heard and he answered. God bless you, my family; God keep you and God touch your lives with his unending love. Love y'all!

My church family—Prosperity Church of God/Prosperity, South Carolina

- Pastors James and Sharonda Chaffins and family
- Pastors Brandon and Rita Crawford and family
- Barry and Debbie Fagin
- Keith and L. Johnson
- Michelle Hancock
- Kathy Williams

Honoring Pastors James and Sharonda Chaffins and Brandon and Rita Crawford—you took on the burden of keeping my finances up to date and current. I know this was a massive undertaking and sacrifice; I can never say thank you enough for your incredible love. I love you!

To my church family, your prayers meant everything to me. I am rich with your kindness and concern: I love each and every one of you!

Newberry County Memorial Hospital—Newberry, South Carolina

To all my nurses, respiratory nurses, occupational and physical therapy nurses, doctors, interns, and kitchen and cleaning staff, God richly bless you all! I am alive today because of the grace of God and your caring hands and heart. God used them to get me back on my feet again! You will not be forgotten!

Amy Silvers, thank you for sneaking in from time to time to check on me. I was not in a place to say how much your actions spoke and how much it meant to me for you to take time out to come just to say, "Hey."

Lovelace Family Medicine—Prosperity, South Carolina

Dr. Oscar Lovelace and all his staff—It was your immediate response and promptness that get me the care and treatment I needed. I know in my heart you went above and beyond what was asked of you. Help came quickly. Had it not been for your assistance, I probably would have been a lot worse off. I am truly grateful. Thank you for your care!

Dr. Pinner Clinic—Peak, South Carolina

Dr. Carroll Pinner and Dr. Edwina Hallman, for all your kindness and care. Thank you and all your wonderful staff. The follow-ups were always delightful and most pleasant. God richly bless you!

Prosperity Police Department—Prosperity, South Carolina

- Chief Wesley Palmore and family
- Sergeant Corey Jones and family
- Corporal Philip Hunter and family
- Officer Jamaurie Gause
- Officer Donald Johnson

Thank you all for your thoughtfulness and concern. Thank you for looking out for me when I was at my worst. I appreciate all that you did, especially when you prayed for me!

Hal and Rita Bowles

I thank you for being there for me. The sacrifice you put in to see that I was taken care of is a debt I will never be able to repay. The miles you put in your vehicles to make sure I had clean clothes. The smiles, the stories, the laughter you gave and gave and gave again. Thank you! Always know that I love you both in Christ Jesus!

The Blend of Art and Coffee

Owners Trent and Kelli Fowler/Kendall Trotter (chef)
A huge thank you! I am blessed to know how much you reached out in my very dark moments of COVID. Thank you for letting me know you were there! Kelli, you just don't realize that the day you said to me, "If you need anything at all, call me and let me know," that statement was profound to me. It may seem simple, but I know your heart was in it, and that was key. May God's love always reside with you and in you, my people at the Blend!
I also thank the *blenders*: Mike Mills, Derek and Shirley Underwood, Zeb and Angela Reid, and family.

Groucho's of Newberry—Newberry, South Carolina

Alexandra Franklin, Maggie White, Sumner Moorer, Trinette Paulsen, Haley Thomason, and James Sims. It is always a blessing to see all your smiling faces and to speak with you. I cherish your friendship always. I greatly thank you for your thoughts, concerns, and prayers: I am blessed to know you all!

Dianna Lynne Design

Owner Dianna Naczi, I count you as my sister in Christ. Struggling through COVID, I never have and never will forget your text messages, constantly and consistently letting me know I was in your prayers. I am thankful for you and your husband moving to our area; I have reaped the rewards of your kind hearts.

Willie Mayes

I appreciate you, my brother. You cannot begin to imagine all that you have done. I hope that I never take for granted your kindness and generosity. You, sir, have a big heart, and I am honored to be a friend, even if you do drive slower than Ms. Daisy! I thank God for you because I see you as my brother. When you caught COVID in 2020, I was genuinely concerned. I was afraid of the worst. I thank God he brought you through it! Love you in Christ, my brother!

Kimberly Smith

I never forgot your kindness. You always had that serious look, ready to help where you could. If I needed anything, you were always willing and fast to make sure I had my needs met. Even though COVID has taken its toll, I didn't forget you. I'm sorry that initially I didn't remember your name but always know that I appreciate your kind and generous heart. God richly bless you and your family!

Beranda Trammell

You are a wonderful friend. You were there when I first came to Prosperity. I always appreciated you as my friend. Thank you for always listening and being there for me when I needed you. Thank you for sharing your tough moments and trusting me with your heart. My appreciation for you is on a grand scale, and I thank God for you. May God bless you always, and may his love extend to those who are very important to you!

Sheena Paige

Lady, you are incredible! The way we met was, by all accounts, almost disastrous, but look what the Lord did. Because of you, I had an angel in my hospital room. God knows how much I appreciate you. You have an incredible heart and vibrant spirit to match; may God's tender mercies always embrace you and those that matter so much to you. Love you in Christ Jesus!

My brothers and sisters in arms in Newberry, South Carolina

- Newberry County Sheriff's Office—Sheriff Lee Foster and all deputies
- Newberry Police Department—Chief Kevin Goodman and all officers
- Whitmire Police Department—Chief Jeremiah Sinclair and all officers
- Rescue Squads in Prosperity, Pomaria, Chappells, Little Mountain, and Whitmire
- To all EMS stations in Newberry County

To the Fire Departments

Prosperity, Whitmire, and City of Newberry Fire Departments— hey, guys. Words are simply not enough. I appreciate everyone who took the time to lift me in prayer. May God richly bless every one of you, your families, and everyone near and dear to your hearts. Thank you!

Prosperity Town Hall

Karen Livingston, Karen Hansel, and Michelle Bundrick, I appreciate your struggle in prayers for me. I am blessed for that sacrifice. I thank God for you and for caring enough to make mention of me in your prayers. Thank you!

Prosperity Town Government

Mayor Derrick Underwood and family, Councilman Allen Gallman, Councilman Chad Hawkins, Councilman Mike Hawkins, and Councilman Robert Martin and family, thank you for your constant concerns and prayers. Gentlemen, God is greater than government; thank you for including me in your busy schedules. I pray to God to bless your endeavors and listen to your cares. May your families prosper in the light of God's gracious love!

Josh and Candice Kingsmore

So many days and nights I received your text messages while I was recovering from COVID. I wish I could have answered them all. You are wonderful friends. Thank you very much for your consistency in caring for me. You guys always made it a point to take time out just to shoot me a message to say, "We are here and we are always thinking of you." As you were faithful in caring for me, God be faithful to you and richly bless your kindness. Thank you!

A special very thanks to:

- On the Square Hair Design—Lori Longshore and staff
- Western Auto staff and family
- Roma's House of Pizza, staff and family
- Robiette Hazel

- Ram Garcia and family
- First Citizens Bank of Prosperity
- First Community Bank of Prosperity
- Food Lion staff

This acknowledgment serves as a reminder of how I am blessed above and beyond anything I could have ever imagined. Each name represents a very unique blessing in my life. Each and every one of you has participated, sacrificed, donated, texted and called me, gave, and unselfishly prayed for me. I am honored; I am overwhelmed!

As many people as I have hurt in my past, the gracious love of God gave me another chance to have friends, and I thank the *Lord* for each of you!

*****

My prayer:

I pray to speak of you, *Lord*, every time you grant me an opportunity.

I pray that you will bless each and every reader and everyone I have mentioned above, their families, and their loved ones and that you may provide them a safe sanctuary as you have provided me, resting in the providence of your awesome and mighty power.

I hope that you, *Lord*, will use my past, a messed up person, as a testimony of your holiness and the hope that can be found only in Jesus Christ. Use me, *Lord*, as an instrument of praise to inspire and encourage those who have read this book. Inspire and encourage the reader to trust you, to hope in you, to believe in you, and to have a relationship with you by getting to know you in your word. I pray that you make yourself real to the reader, whoever it may be.

Thank you, Jesus; because of you, I have hope. Thank you for taking my place on the cross. Thank you for dying for me. My sufferings have testified of your great love. Thank you, *Lord*. I am eternally grateful!

To God be all praise, and honor, and power, and glory, both now and forever…by the power of the Holy Spirit…in Jesus's name I pray. Amen!

For God so loved the world…

—Yeshua

About the Author

He was born in San Antonio, Texas and was raised in Lockhart, where he graduated high school in 1984. The author moved to South Carolina in 2000. In 2006, he graduated from the South Carolina Criminal Justice Academy as a Class I law enforcement officer. He enjoys the company of great friends and spends his time in the continual pursuit of his faith in Christ.